PRAISE FOR

# HER BRAVE JOURNEY

"The most important thing we can do to end intimate partner violence is to break the silence. Sharing stories that uplift the realities of survivors can end the stigma, especially in underrepresented communities. Swati Singh shines a light on a public health crisis that lives in the shadows. *Her Brave Journey* will empower survivors and remind them that they are not alone."

—RACHNA KHARE, Executive Director, Daya, and
    IRFANA HUSSAIN, Director of Outreach & Education, Daya ,
    www.dayahouston.org

"Raw and real, Swati Singh's first novel is a true inspiration!
    "Each of us looks at the world through our own cultural lens, molded by parenting, education, economics, politics, religion, and personality. This is a book of profound hardship buffeted by the drive to survive, a rocky journey to a destination of kindness, generosity, and forgiveness . . . met with success by a brave, intelligent, and strong woman. A hero of her time."

—CHINA CAY CROSS AND LINDA CROSS, Editors

"*Her Brave Journey* is more than a provocative story about courage, resilience, and personal empowerment. It also unabashedly forces us to take stock of who we are, and for men especially is a searing reminder of how much work remains, on ourselves, and in how we treat women."

—MICHAEL J. COFFINO, Author of *Truth Is in the House* and Co-author of
    *Play It Forward: From Gymboree to the Yoga Mat and Beyond*

"*Her Brave Journey* is a bold and unapologetically soul-baring read that aligns with the author's mission to give voice to those who need to be heard."

—CHELA HARDY, Publishing Consultant, AskChela

"Swati Singh does an admirable job painting a personal picture of a woman facing a life-altering decision. *Her Brave New Journey* is a must read for any person amid rebuilding their lives after a traumatic breakup."

—MILDRED ANTENOR, Author of *The Gladioli Are Invisible: A Memoir*

"In *Her Brave Journey*, Swati Singh introduces Kiara, a young woman of Indian descent, who finds herself in an unhealthy marriage. As Kiara contemplates how to move forward, she realizes her personal values contradict with the cultural and societal beliefs she was raised with. Readers will cheer for Kiara as they witness her growing stronger by accessing spiritual and mental health guidance. Now self-empowered, Kiara chooses her life path with confidence and hope"

—JOAN HICKS BOONE, Author of *The Best Girl*

"Debut author Swati Singh tackles a sensitive subject as she gains inner strength through spirituality. On her 'brave journey' she learns timeless lessons that can be applied to all aspects of life. Singh's words speak empowerment and strength. Bravo."

—BENJAMIN BERKLEY, Author of *Against My Will* and *In Defense of Guilt*

"Singh's compelling novel takes the reader through the history of a complex relationship through the eyes of a unique protagonist. As a criminal defense attorney who has handled these types of cases for years from the defense side, I learned a lot from this novel. Kiara is a heroine people will cheer for and remember!"

—CHRIS LEIBIG, Criminal Defense Attorney and Award-winning Author of *Almost Mortal*

"Though she didn't know about narcissism, Kiara knew if she didn't leave her husband, he would kill her. Swati Singh's *Her Brave Journey* describes a bad marriage, an abusive man, a compliant woman, and her journey into personal strength as she discovers the power of forgiveness"

—B. LYNN GOODWIN, Author of *Talent* and *Never Too Late: From Wannabe to Wife at 62*

"*Her Brave Journey* exemplifies the courage, determination and growth it takes for a woman to leave an abusive relationship. Kiara was a woman with a loving and forgiving nature who forgave her husband over and over again after he abused her. She fully believed his promises of never hurting her again and gave so much of herself in the marriage. I loved being able to feel Kiara's emotions and to see her learning to love herself as much as she had always loved others."

—MARI MITCHELL, Dare to be Authentic Coaching

"An impactful and compelling story about a woman's ability to continually find herself even through adversity. An inspiration to those who are stuck in bad relationships and ideals of culture and tradition."

—Bridget O'Brien, CEO Bridget O'Brien PR & Events

"A beautifully written story about the defining moments in life and love, even when they may not be what is expected. Swati Singh's powerful storytelling offers insight into how expectations influence people."

—KELLY FITZPATRICK, Founding Member, Board Member of USA Irish Dance Alliance

"A sympathetic and inspired story of a young lady's ability to empower herself and be her own hero."

—EILEEN FARRELL, Fashion Tech Designer

*Her Brave Journey*
by Swati Singh

© Copyright 2021 Swati Singh

ISBN 978-1-64663-140-7

This is a work of fiction. The characters are both actual and fictitious. With the exception of verified historical events and persons, all incidents, descriptions, dialogue and opinions expressed are the products of the author's imagination and are not to be construed as real.

Published by

 köehlerbooks™

3705 Shore Drive
Virginia Beach, VA 23455
800-435-4811
www.koehlerbooks.com

# Her Brave Journey

SWATI SINGH

VIRGINIA BEACH
CAPE CHARLES

# TABLE OF CONTENTS

# *Speaking to my younger self*

"You will face many defeats in your life, but never let
yourself be defeated"

**—Maya Angelou**

I have been in the care of a wonderful therapist and as part of that care, she asked me to close my eyes and pretend we were in a park with a playground, children in the distance playing, laughing, and enjoying themselves. My therapist asked me to picture myself there, I see myself sitting alone on a park bench, I am about 8 or 9, I am drawing with a pencil on a pad of paper. My head is down . . . I look sad and lonely.

"Speak to that child, Kiara," my therapist said. "I would like you to have a conversation with her sharing your experiences at her age and older and sharing what you have learned over the years that helped lessen the sadness. Sharing your story will help and she is waiting for you . . . Talk to her from your heart."

I walked over to the bench and sat down beside her. She was drawing figures that even in her untrained effort, resembled a group of girls on and around the swings; they were playing together and having a good time.

I felt a pain in my heart as I recognized her sadness. Immediately I recalled the feelings of loneliness imposed by separation from the group and feeling invisible to them.

"Talk to her, Kiara," my therapist directed. "Open your heart and say all of the things you would like your younger self to know about what she is going through now and what she will go through in the future. Assure her that everything will be okay. Comfort her. Let her see the confident, secure, and wise woman you have become. Share with her what you have learned. It will help so very much. Tell her the things you would have liked to have known."

I listened to my therapist's words and looked at my younger self and suddenly I wanted nothing more than to ease her pain and lighten her worries. I wanted to share with her how bright her future would be.

"Kiara, I am the grown-up you. I have been with you over the years and am with you now as you experience hurt feelings, prejudices, and injustices.

"I want to tell you about some of the experiences you will have because I have lived them. I also want to take this opportunity to apologize to you for so many things you will have to go through because of my lack of understanding when I was your age. I did not know things would get better, but they did. Let me assure you now, that your future will turn out to be wonderful. Your life story will be a rollercoaster with lots of highs and lows and you will rarely get things in life easily. Most of the time you will end up getting what your heart desires, but you will go through many trials and tribulations just to get what you want.

You will often face rejection, criticism, and pushback on your first attempts. Again, you will eventually get what you want but it will only be after several efforts. It is a tough pill to swallow, but this is your reality. I know it is difficult to believe today, but gradually you will grow from a shy and timid child into a sassy, confident and resilient woman."

"Although you will have your share of tough moments during your younger days, there is a bright and happy future ahead of you. You will be a late bloomer in many respects. There will be several moments of hitting rock bottom, but you will bounce back each time.

"As an adult, people will say you are cold-hearted, unapproachable, and that you have a wall around yourself. People know who you are, but not your stories. You will have to confront and fight off many inner demons and insecurities. Regardless, one big life lesson I can teach you is this: You will be the only problem you will ever have, and you will be the only solution. You must believe in yourself.

"I know you are bullied in school. You deal with so many kids who insult you, push you around, and make you cry daily. When those school kids say you are unworthy, unwanted, and unlovable, you believe them. I know it hurts. When they say you are good for nothing and have no future, again - you believe them. I am so sorry we thought they were right. They are not right. What you have not understood just yet is that bullies are extremely insecure people and only pick on those who they perceive as vulnerable and pickable. That is their problem, not yours.

"You think that turning the other cheek is what sweet and nice girls are supposed to do. I wish I had known that was not right. I should have shared what was happening with my teachers, parents, and big sisters about the bullies. I am sorry that I did not ask for help.

"Although the years of being a teenager and a young adult will be filled with insecurities, your mid-twenties will be much better, and you will transform yourself into a successful positive woman.

"Later as an adult, you will be compelled to write a list of "Life Lessons Learned". You will write this when life has really been tough; and the list will be full of anger and the hurt you are feeling and that you will build upon as you continue to experience cruelty and prejudice. Please know that not all people are against you. In fact, few people are . . . and most are not mean. That all unhappy people want others to be unhappy too. That is mostly not true. Perhaps other people misunderstand you or perhaps you misunderstand them. You will learn not to give up on people. People are basically good, Kiara.

The grown-up Kiara studied her younger self as she spoke . . . "You are a beautiful and loving person. Please learn to trust as many people as you can with your soul and your heart. Try not to judge others. Most people are insecure and just want to be accepted. Like you. You will learn that it is a big world, with many joys to experience. Strive to be happy."

"And I know, even at your age you worry about your family. There is no need to worry. It will turn out that you and your big sisters will be remarkable daughters to your parents and will be the caretakers for your entire family.

"You will be fulfilled with your career, family, and friendships. You will travel to amazing places like Spain, England, Mexico, India, and the Bahamas and you will live in many places outside of your hometown.

"This may surprise you now, but you will please everyone with your sly and stunning sense of humor! Friends, family, and coworkers will describe your sense of humor as cynical and snarky but not mean. This can be entertaining and endearing, and many people will want to be around you. You will meet several celebrities, reality stars and even be on *The Price is Right!* Above all, you will accomplish your lifetime ambition (what some called *a lofty dream*) of publishing a book!

"Most of the hardships you will experience ahead, are mainly due to tough circumstances or bad decisions. It will take a lot of inner strength and resilience to deal with these challenges, but you have it all within you! You are a survivor!

"I know it feels so scary but please do not be fearful of the unknown. It may be hard for you to believe this, but one day a lot of women will recognize you as a source of inspiration to them. You have a beautiful future, and you will be proud of the fiercely kind and wonderful woman you grow up to be. Remember, you are the only problem you will ever have, *and* you will be the only solution. I am immensely proud of you!"

• •

Kiara opened her eyes at the bidding of her therapist and looked around. She was almost shocked to find she was in an office, her face wet with tears, and not still sitting on the park bench feeling the sun.

"Kiara, how do you feel? Did you find it helpful to go back and talk to your younger self?"

Kiara smiled at her therapist and said with great emotion: "OH I really loved seeing the younger me. —If only I knew then what I know now . . ."

# CHAPTER ONE

# Pursuit of Life, Liberty, and Happiness

"Do what you feel in your heart to be right—
for you'll be criticized anyway"

**—Eleanor Roosevelt**

He held her head so aggressively against the bed's headboard that her neck twisted and she could not move. The few seconds when she did try catching her breath, all she kept saying was, "Please do not kill me, my parents need me. Please, Angad, I can't breathe, don't kill me. I'm begging you; my parents need me." Fighting to breathe, her voice was hoarse and almost robotic from the strangulation.

Pinned on top of her, his teeth were grinding, and his body shook with anger as he continued strangling and screaming, "You bitch! You only care about your family! What about me?! You don't care about me at all!"

Her life was completely at the mercy of her husband. For some reason, the more she said those words, "My parents need me, please don't kill me," the stronger he got. Her entire life flashed before her eyes. During those almost-final moments, the only images Kiara saw were of her mother and father.

Finally, she gasped, "I love you, Angad. Please do not kill me. I love you." After hearing those words, he stopped suddenly.

The next morning while getting ready for work, Kiara stared at her bruises in the bathroom mirror. *What happened to me yesterday? How did I reach this point in my life? The man who claims to love me almost killed me. What a foolish woman I am.*

Angad was taking Kiara to the train station where she had an hour-long commute to work in mid-town Manhattan from their home in Stamford, Connecticut. During that day's commute, she was silent and not interested in talking to Angad at all. She could not believe that her husband beat her the previous day. While on the train, Kiara kept visualizing her entire life and the events leading her up to this day in June 2010. Kiara's thoughts kept swirling during what felt like the longest commute of her life. *How did I get here? What have I done wrong to get a beating from a man who says he loves me?* Her mind took her down memory lane as she tried so hard to understand how her journey had brought her to this present day.

Kiara was born in South India and immigrated to the United States in 1980 at five years old with her parents and two older sisters. They settled in the suburbs of Sacramento, California. She grew up in an extremely strict, conservative, and patriarchal Hindu household where daughters were expected to be obedient, quiet, and follow the rules. Although she and her sisters had very loving and strong relationships with their parents, they were restricted from dating, wearing short dresses and skirts, and having any social life outside of school. A typical middle-class Indian American household back in those days would expect their daughters to finish high school or college, have an arranged marriage, produce children, be a stay-at-home mom, and continue this same cycle of life with their own children. Naturally, Kiara developed this same mindset and thought she would also follow this so-called cycle of life.

Apart from being strict, her family was also deeply religious. Her mother, aunts, sisters, and older cousins always fasted on Hindi holidays and prayed for the wellbeing of the men of the family. In the Hindu culture, it is a practice for women to fast and pray for their husbands, brothers, sons, and sons-in-law. Single women were required to fast and pray to God for a future suitable husband. So, starting right from childhood, Kiara was conditioned to believe that men hold the power and women stood back and listened.

By nature, Kiara was a shy, timid child, so she was constantly a target for bullies. In school, the other kids made fun of her dark skin, called her *fruit-by-the-foot* because of her short height, accused her of not showering because she supposedly smelled like curry, mocked her Indian accent, labeled her "the little Indian girl" and other racist names. She was always the odd one out, who never got invited to birthday parties and was left out of group activities during recess and in the classroom. It was easy for bullies to beat her up and make her cry because she appeared physically fragile and emotionally vulnerable. She was so obedient and always did what others told her to do because she thought that good girls were supposed to be sweet, gentle, and turn the other cheek.

Despite her childhood insecurities, Kiara outshined the others in dancing and playing sports. Without taking classes, Kiara was naturally a particularly good dancer and loved performing to Bollywood songs in front of large audiences. Kiara was also very athletic and competitive. Considering her petite size and lack of popularity, Kiara was always the last one picked to be on a team in sports. However, once she got on the basketball court, soccer field, and hockey field, she kicked everyone's ass. While the other girls were too scared to compete with the boys, Kiara was the only girl who dared to play floor hockey with them during gym class and ended up crushing the competition every time. Even on the basketball court when the other kids left her out, she just grabbed a ball and played alone. Out of the fifty kids playing, the only student the gym teacher was impressed by was her.

Judged by the other kids as frail, Kiara's patience was constantly tested by those kids pulling her hair, lifting her dress, throwing pencils at her, and stealing her food. What they did not know was that deep down in her heart, Kiara had a fierce fighting spirit, which she herself did not recognize. Once during a kickball game when a mean white girl pushed and hit her, Kiara grabbed the girl's head, pulled her hair, and scratched her face. In another instance in the classroom one day, Kiara fought back when another mean girl tried stabbing her hand with a pencil. Kiara grabbed that girl's hair, gave her neck a whiplash, and scraped her hand with that same pencil.

Despite being harassed so much in school every day, Kiara still did not tell her parents, older sisters, or teachers about it because she thought that sweet and nice girls were not supposed to tattletale. Constantly being bullied, she grew up to be extremely insecure as a teenager and even as a young adult.

By the time Kiara reached the age of twenty in 1995, she had an arranged marriage. Her parents had the most honorable intentions in mind when setting up this marriage; to them, it was their parental duty to secure a husband for their daughter. All the women in her family, including her sisters, were also subject to arranged marriages. Even if some of those women were not completely happy, they compromised because they were conditioned to think that marriage was the ultimate destiny for women. Arranged marriages were— and to a certain extent still are—a big part of the Indian culture. If anyone dared to have a divorce, they were commonly outcast by their family and the rest of Indian society. Divorce was considered the ultimate betrayal to a family's honor and reputation, regardless of how miserable the woman was.

But after getting married, things became difficult for Kiara because she just could not accept the man she had been arranged with, as she was not in love with him. They were not compatible on any level and could not even consummate the marriage. The pressures of compromising with an unhappy marriage began taking a toll on her. By the age of twenty-two, Kiara hit rock bottom psychologically, emotionally, and financially. After crying herself to sleep every night, she finally realized that enough was enough; she no longer wanted to be an obedient woman.

On December 28, 1997, she told her husband (who at that point was more like a roommate) that she could not continue being trapped in an unhappy marriage. For the first time, she wanted independence, freedom, and a normal social life like other women her age. After much deliberation, she realized that the first step to freedom was to risk severely hurting and disappointing her family by divorcing the stranger she was married to and reclaiming her independence.

Kiara knew the word divorce was extremely taboo and that she would probably be stigmatized after making this decision. Divorcing in those circumstances was also difficult as hell because Kiara was studying in graduate school, so she had little savings, a low-paying job, no personal resources, and no self-esteem. She would have no guarantees in life. She had grown up completely dependent on others, so she did not have street smarts or the practical experience of being on her own.

With the odds stacked against her, it was extremely difficult for a timid and vulnerable woman like Kiara to move forward with the big decision of getting a divorce, especially at this age. Nonetheless, she pulled herself together, filed for divorce at age twenty-two, moved back in with her parents, and vowed to change her life.

First, she needed a better-paying job. She did not, however, have the professional skills to even go on major job interviews. As a person, she was so emotionally scarred and psychologically damaged by the insecurities in her life that she even cried during a few of the job interviews. She received a lot of compassion from those potential employers, but not a job.

After several heartbreaking rejections, Kiara finally landed a decent paying job as a head-hunter at a staffing agency. Kiara genuinely did not understand how a person like her who cried during job interviews managed to get a job as a head-hunter where she now had to interview other candidates for jobs. How did she make it to the other side of the table? --This would be the first time Kiara learned to, not only fake it 'til you make it, but fake it 'til you become it.

This job turned out to be not only a stepping-stone into a real career, but it symbolized the beginning of her *personal pursuit of life, liberty, and happiness.* After she turned twenty-three in 1998, she began her self-discovery and breakthrough years.

At work, she observed how the strong and powerful women behaved and she wanted to be just like them. One woman in particular named Natasha was someone Kiara envied and wanted to copy. Natasha was also South Asian and Kiara's age, so they had these things in common; however, there was a night and day difference in their personalities. While Kiara was new to this company and still learning how to carry herself, Natasha had worked there for years and had established strong relationships with everyone. When she walked by, men stood up and stared at her. When she walked into the room, she owned it and made heads turn. Natasha was fierce, outspoken, confident, and very stylish. Kiara observed Natasha's mannerisms, social etiquette, and "fashionista" style and became so inspired by those qualities that she began teaching herself of those traits.

Gradually, Kiara started making milestone improvements in herself physically, emotionally, professionally, and financially. One by one, Kiara learned how to build her professional skills and social street-smarts through work. With the little savings she had, she began improving her physical appearance by joining the gym, eating healthier, and eventually losing thirty pounds.

Kiara upgraded her wardrobe style, switched to colored contacts, bought fancy make-up and shoes, and practiced how to walk in high heels. Fed up with social anxiety, she deliberately challenged herself to attend parties, happy hours, conferences, and networking events. Because of these events, she was motivated to work even harder on her career, looks, social skills, personality, and self-esteem, --not only to impress others, but primarily to impress herself. Going outside of her comfort zone, Kiara developed self-confidence; she was more social, expressed her thoughts eloquently, and built a strong professional network.

After turning twenty-five in 2000, Kiara even graduated with her master's degree in Business Administration from California State University, which in and of itself was an enormous achievement. Finishing graduate school while simultaneously working full-time gave Kiara a big self-esteem boost that she desperately needed. This achievement helped her recognize her inner strengths, intelligence, and her ability to "get the job done."

The same girl who was shy and timid her whole life was now developing into a sassy, outspoken, and confident young woman. The same girl who was scared to push back at bullies was now a fierce woman who did not tolerate bullying from anyone! She did a complete one-eighty from the girl she used to be and blossomed into a stunningly fierce and powerful woman with strong opinions and language, and an unfiltered sense of humor. Even in the workplace, Kiara learned how to lead meetings, give presentations, and speak up for herself.

After a few years of working as a head-hunter, Kiara switched careers from staffing to marketing. Thanks to all the experience she gained from training candidates on job interviews, Kiara learned the art of networking, job interviews, and negotiating a high salary. By the age of thirty in 2005, she landed a terrific position with a Fortune 500 marketing company in downtown Sacramento, where she had a fancy office with a clear view of the waterfront. This job required her to travel nationwide, give PowerPoint presentations at conferences, and network with influencers.

Another thing Kiara learned while in this position, was the art of confrontation. Her direct manager, Chris, had a reputation for being a bully to everyone in the company, and she experienced his hostile behavior the most because they worked so closely together. Before switching careers to marketing, he was a restaurant manager and had gotten by with speaking to staff in a hostile manner.

He constantly took out his work frustrations on Kiara, threw a folder on the floor towards her during a meeting, talked over her, and blatantly disrespected her in front of others. Because he was her boss, she ignored his hostility several times until she finally got into a heated argument where she shouted, "I am *not* your server from Applebee's!" Her co-workers were all shocked and impressed by how Kiara assertively defended herself to the office bully. She was the only one who had the courage to stand up to Chris. She then formally complained about him to Human Resources.

He never dared to talk down to Kiara again. As someone who was too scared to fight bullies her entire life, Kiara was finally learning how to fearlessly push back and defend herself, even against authority figures. After this incident, she gained so much respect from her workplace that nobody ever dared to get on her bad side. Her career was going so well that she felt like she was on cloud nine.

And her social life had become extremely exciting. Through all these networking events and parties, she found a great circle of friends and even vacationed in London, Cancun, and the Bahamas with them. Not only did Kiara establish amazing friendships and professional connections with influencers, but eventually she began dating as well.

# CHAPTER TWO

# *"The Turning Point"*

"When you judge another, you do not define them.
You define yourself."

—**Wayne Dyer**

After her divorce was final, Kiara began casually dating. Since she never even consummated her marriage, she came out of that relationship as a virginal divorcee. Going out to parties and social gatherings every night really helped her self-confidence when it came to knowing how to carry herself around men. After casually dating, Kiara finally lost her virginity at age twenty-three. However, the man she ended up losing her virginity to was awkward and had no social skills at all! When he spoke, he mumbled. She barely understood what he said.

Surprisingly, Mr. Awkward was quite experienced and taught her various sexual positions; he knew exactly how to "put the key in the ignition". Although her first sexual experience was fun and amazing all around, was she shocked to see an ejaculation for the first time. She did not know how the process of masturbation worked, so the first time she saw the outcome, she thought to herself, *What just happened to his body?* Mr. Awkward did not even give her a warning!

So, anyone could imagine her confusion. --She could not tell if he was in pain or pleasure; even his facial expressions confused her!

Growing up in such an uptight family, Kiara and her sisters were not even allowed to say the word "sex" in front of parents or siblings. Even during health class in school, the topic of sex was thought to be too taboo for her prudish and virginal eyes and ears. Kiara had been naïve and ignorant about the process of how sex worked. But now --finally dating, she eventually realized that she brought so much pleasure to this man and was immensely proud of herself for breaking this ice. After some time, she understood that sex would take some practice, so Kiara continued this exhilarating adventure, enthusiastically. Romantically socializing with men felt so fresh and exciting that she would go on multiple dates every few weeks with a new man she had just met. No, she did not sleep with all of them, but it was very sexy and flattering to get attention and have men pursue her for the first time.

At that time, Kiara was just having fun dating random men because she had this newfound freedom and felt sexually liberated for the first time in her life. But she just never took any of those men seriously. In fact, whenever one man was in town to visit, she spent the night with him at his hotel. Then, the next night, she went on a second date with a different man she met the previous week. During one of those dates, she almost had a quickie in the car with another pathetic guy, but he seemed like just a walking penis with no aim! After that, she stopped taking his calls. What a lousy waste of time!

While some of these dates were okay, the majority were a bit strange. Kiara met up with one date at a restaurant. He showed up looking like he just rolled out of bed with a wrinkled shirt, messy hair, and mismatched socks. He sat right next to her in the booth and proceeded to slide a butter knife up and down her thigh. After dinner, he walked her to the car and leaned to her kiss her but jammed his tongue right inside her mouth and kept it still. It was the stupidest kiss she ever had!

Another guy that she met at a party, told her that he just got out of a long-term relationship, so he was not looking for a commitment. Instead, he asked if he could be her maintenance man as she observed him stroking his penis through his jeans. During another date, she went out with a guy who kept interrupting her every time she talked.

Being the impatient person Kiara was, after the third or fourth time he interrupted her, she finally asked him, "Do you want to hear anything I have to say?"

He apologized profusely and said, "You are right. I am so sorry!" Then he pulled out a pad of paper and a pen and jotted notes as she continued telling him about herself. Kiara asked him what he was doing, and he said, "Oh, I am writing down things I want to tell you when it is my turn to finally talk again."

After that came a string of more nightmare dates. For example, leaving an insect festival (how romantic!) early because her date's *wife* showed up, and another man who took her to a haunted house but left her there because he got scared.

One day in June 2005, Kiara flew to Washington, DC, to attend an international work conference located at the Ronald Reagan Building. Here, Kiara began to think her luck might be changing. Directly beside her table was the table of an international marketing firm from Tel Aviv, Israel. Kiara saw a handsome and very tall man at that table talking to others. He wore a chic black suit, had thick dark black hair, and was athletically built. Right when she set her eyes on him, her jaw dropped, and she could not stop staring at him. She was so distracted by this sexy, attractive man that she could not pay attention to her own table. She had only seen good-looking men like him in movies and was completely in lust.

As he was working, she tried awfully hard to get his attention by fixing her body posture, twirling her hair, and undressing him with her eyes. Finally, he looked at her and understood she was flirting with him through her eyes, hair, and body language. Standing tall with both hands in his pocket, he gave her a seductive stare and winked. She could feel the sexual tension from across the room. Living in the moment, she could not pass up the opportunity to talk to this gorgeous gentleman. Kiara boldly walked up to him and introduced herself.

"Hello, I'm Kiara," she said.

"Hi, Kiara, I'm Jacob. Nice to meet you," he said with a very sexy Arabic accent.

"So, what exactly does your company do?" she asked.

He replied, "It is my own business, and I have been running it for ten years now. We help students and student athletes from Israel get placed in universities abroad so they can pursue higher education."

"Oh nice! I previously worked in campus recruitment for years and love working with college students. I switched careers to marketing and communications. Is this your first trip to Washington, DC? How long are you in town?" she asked.

"No, this is my third trip to DC. I come here every couple of years as I do some work with the White House as well. I am in town for another two days," he said.

"I would love to see you before you head back to Israel. Are you free to meet up for drinks tonight?" she asked.

"Yes, I would love that," he said.

"Great. I am staying at the Hyatt Regency near Pennsylvania Avenue. Why don't you meet me in my lobby around 7 p.m.?" she replied. They exchanged business cards.

"Perfect. I'll be there by 7 tonight," Jacob said.

That evening, she anxiously and excitedly got ready for her hot date. Luckily, she packed her sexy black pencil skirt, so she wore that with a tight, low-cut black blouse and black spaghetti-strapped high heels. Jacob arrived and found Kiara waiting for him in the lobby. He greeted her with a peck on her cheek, and they walked over to the hotel bar for drinks. Both talked, laughed, and drank for a few hours. She learned that he was a former basketball player who represented Israel at the International level. He also talked about his military experience since it was legally required for all men and women to join the Israeli military once they reached the age of eighteen.

She was really impressed by his experience as a businessman, a basketball player, and being in the military. No wonder he looked so toned and athletic. On top of that, he had the sexiest Arabic accent. They shamelessly flirted with each other as Jacob kept caressing her legs and neck and she reciprocated. After a few drinks, they took the elevator to her floor and walked into her suite. She knew that inviting a stranger to her room could lead to horrible things like, murder or rape but, for some reason, she felt she could trust this man. Luckily, she was right. As they looked out the large window at the view of the White House and Capitol Building, Jacob stood behind her, and began kissing her neck.

This night ended up being the most seductive rendezvous she had ever had.

The next morning when Kiara woke up, she found Jacob no longer in the room. She thought it was rude of him to leave before at least saying goodbye. Kiara went online to see what more she could find out about him and came across one of his interviews. Shockingly, Kiara noticed he was wearing a wedding band in that video. *Was he a married man?! He did not wear a band yesterday.* She realized that she should have done more research before meeting up with him but was not thinking that far ahead. She was irritated by this whole thing but decided not to reach out to him for clarification. Realistically, what were the chances of her seeing him again anyway? Besides, they both used each other for sex, unemotionally. She treated this date as a one-night fling with a man she would never see again.

Kiara firmly closed this dating chapter and moved on. Life was going incredibly well, just until 2006, when she met a man named, Angad. The expression, *People come into your life for a reason, season, or lifetime,* fit in well with their story. In retrospect, Angad should have only come into her life for a season, but she committed herself to what she thought would be a lifetime—and she will spend the rest of her life trying to understand the reason.

# CHAPTER THREE

# The Power of Persuasion

"If you look up 'charming' in the dictionary,
you will see that it not only has references to strong
attraction, but to spells and magic. Then again,
what are liars if not great magicians?"

**—Deb Caletti**

A t age thirty-one in 2006, Kiara met Angad through a professional, legitimate dating website. She was not having any luck with the men she met offline, so a friend suggested she try something different. The concept of online dating was completely new to her, and most of those dates she went on were a nightmare. Even with the couple of great dates she had, there were issues—they ended up ghosting her. She was beginning to feel discouraged and low. After reviewing some terrible profiles and going on even worse dates, she found Angad's profile to be interesting and wanted to get to know him better. They contacted each other, talked on the phone frequently, and made plans to meet up. She noticed that he was great about staying in touch with her, a trait the other men lacked. But with him, it was different because he was so great about calling, texting, and emailing when he said he would.

The first time they met, he flew from San Francisco to Sacramento to see her. Kiara found him to be exceedingly kind and gracious, and it felt like she had known him her whole life. By nature, he was very shy, soft spoken, and polite, which came off as extremely sweet and charming to people who met him. Angad was 5ft 10, which was a good height for her standing at 5ft 3. Professionally, he worked as a paralegal for a small law firm in San Francisco and was preparing to study for the LSAT. Kiara travelled frequently to San Francisco to visit Angad, meet some of his family and friends and toured the city. When meeting his aunt for the first time, she told Kiara, "Angad is such a kind-hearted soul. He will never hurt anyone." Kiara felt so assured by her words.

During their first date in San Francisco, he took her see the Golden Gate Bridge, Alcatraz Island, and Napa Valley. She had never visited this city before, so it was nice touring it for the first time with him.

Gradually, both got to know each other better and soon became particularly good friends. Kiara told him all about her personal history and family background. She was a very transparent and outspoken woman who wore her heart on her sleeve. She felt like she could trust him, so she told him about her insecurities, vulnerabilities, mistakes, and life lessons learned. He appreciated her transparency and assured her that she should not feel insecure anymore because he was here now, for her.

After listening to Kiara's life stories, he told her his.

Angad was born and raised in India in a middle-class family. Despite middle-class circumstances, his parents put him through the best Catholic schools in the upscale neighborhoods of New Delhi. He had ambitious dreams of moving up in life financially, professionally, and socially. Angad was very studious, and because of his outstanding grades in school, he received an F1 student visa to pursue higher education in the United States.

His family background was interesting and unconventional. He lived in a joint family with his parents, younger sister, grandparents, uncles, aunts, and nephew. Angad had a good relationship with all the family members he lived with and was a very respectful son. The household was a typical traditional Indian family where the men worked and oversaw the bills and the women cooked, cleaned, and were the last ones to eat the food they cooked. Although his mother and father had a strong and healthy bond with each other, his uncle and aunt did not. His uncle was very narcissistic, chauvinistic, and angry. Because he was one of the breadwinners of the family, he asserted full power and control over everyone, especially his wife. When he talked, she listened quietly.

His uncle's lifestyle also was not healthy. He was an alcoholic and occasionally brought home prostitutes. Although Angad was never abused himself, he witnessed his uncle physically and verbally abusing his aunt on a regular basis. It was common for his uncle to come home past midnight drunk, and sexually and physically abuse his wife. Sometimes her resistance and crying would be so loud that Angad would wake up to the terrible noises coming from their room.

Angad was present for many of these violent scenes, including the time he saw his uncle grab his aunt by the hair and swing her head so hard that she fell on the floor in a fetal position. Another time, his uncle grabbed his aunt by the throat, dragged her into the next room and then slapped her so hard that she could not stop wailing. Initially watching their violence scared Angad, but this became the new normal in their house.

The most horrifying of these instances that Angad witnessed, however, came on a night his uncle had brought home another prostitute. His wife, a woman who had suffered her husband's violence and infidelity for so long, had gone beyond her limit and could no longer tolerate his behavior. In the middle of the night, Angad heard a lot of commotion from the kitchen. His grandmother who usually slept next to him, was not in bed. He was used to hearing the violent noises in the house, but these noises sounded different.

Slowly he walked to the hallway and into the kitchen and saw his aunt pouring gasoline on herself. His family members were trying to stop her. Angad quickly grabbed his cousin to keep him safe, but shortly after that, his aunt lit a match on herself and burned to death. She was so fed up with the abuse that she could not think of any other solution than committing suicide. It was the most gruesome scene any human, let alone a child, could witness.

Angad went on to tell Kiara these stories and how the visual of his aunt burning herself to death would stay in his mind forever. He also talked to her about his resentment towards his parents. As a child, Angad nagged his parents almost constantly to move out of that abusive household, but they did not because they believed families should all live jointly under the same roof. Angad resented his parents because of the trauma he suffered as a child. He felt completely neglected and abandoned by them.

Angad also went on to tell Kiara about a previous relationship he was in. Before meeting Kiara, he was engaged to a woman from his community in New Delhi. One day, he found out she cheated on him, and it took an exceedingly long time for him to recover from the hurt. Angad felt so neglected and abandoned by the important people in his life that he was afraid to trust anyone.

When he told Kiara all these disturbing stories, she became very emotional. She was so impressed by how Angad got himself out of that toxic household, came to the United States with help from no one, and was now focusing on his career. He was living the American dream and was a great example of a self-made immigrant. After hearing his story, she felt a sense of responsibility and affection towards him. She never met a man who was so sensitive and kind-hearted.

Just two months into dating, Angad told Kiara he was in love with her and wanted to marry her. This was the first time a man said, "I love you," and her heart immediately melted. She never thought she would meet a man who treated her so affectionately, and she had fallen for his gentle and charming personality. He knew her history and understood her insecurities well. He would say things such as, "I do not care about any of your issues from the past. I just know I want to be with you. And if anyone in society points their finger at you or criticizes you about anything, they will have to answer to me."

They exchanged emails daily. Angad would say things to her like, "Kiara, I completely understand your insecurities. But I assure you, if you give me a chance, I promise you a very bright and happy future with me. I want to go to law school because I want to move up professionally and financially. I will give you such a happy life. I do not want to pressure you, if you still are uncomfortable, I completely understand and will respect your decision to go separate ways if that is what you want."

Kiara was touched by his kind words. She felt respected and loved and found herself warming up to the idea of marriage. A few months later, he traveled to Sacramento to meet her family. She had never introduced a man to her family; this was a completely new experience for her and them. He was genuinely respectful and so charming that they immediately loved him.

He told her dad, "Please do not worry. I will take particularly good care of Kiara. You have nothing to worry about." He also immediately formed an adorable friendship with her nieces and even offered to pay for their college tuition. After getting the stamp of approval from her immediate family, she gradually introduced him to her friends and extended family. Everyone admired his professional ambitions, and they were impressed by his sweet and sincere personality.

People would even joke that Angad was too nice for Kiara and how she was lucky to find a guy like him. So flattered was she by their compliments and approvals that she felt like marrying him was the right decision. If there was a day when Angad did not hear from Kiara, he would say things such as, "I feel like a fish out of water when we do not talk." As cheesy as it sounded, she thought it was cute.

During those days, Angad was applying to law schools on the East Coast since those schools ranked Tier One. Kiara was impressed by his ambitious nature and helped him day and night by researching good schools, salary data, and lucrative internships. As a marketing influencer, Kiara had a strong network of professional connections. She introduced Angad to her entire professional network, edited his essays, conducted mock interviews, and put together his resume and cover letters. There were days when they sat together with their respective laptops and did nothing but research law schools, pitched Angad's resume, and cold-called companies for work-study internship programs.

Most of their meetups and conversations revolved around Angad's career, schedule, and financial prosperity. It felt like Kiara suddenly became his career counselor and agent. But since they talked about eventually getting married, she built her future around his plans and was determined to help him succeed in his law career. One day he even told her, "You know, Kiara, people always say that behind a successful man is a strong woman. When I investigate my future, I see you as the woman behind my success." She was so flattered by his words. She began daydreaming about being the wife of a successful corporate attorney.

Because Angad was in the process of switching careers and saving up for law school, he was incredibly careful about his monthly budget, so she stepped up and pitched in towards some of his expenses. For example, she bought him a fancy professional suit, a high-tech laptop, and even paid for his aptitude exams and school applications. Financially, Kiara was doing extremely well and had a happy and successful career. Yes, the bills she helped Angad with were piling up, but she thought that big sacrifices brought big rewards. To Kiara, putting her time and money into this relationship would reap a good return someday. Things in their relationship were going so well that she was completely smitten and on cloud nine.

One thing Kiara was very upfront about to Angad was that she wanted to stay in California after marriage. She was perfectly fine with relocating out of state if he was admitted to a law school outside of her home state. But after graduation, she wanted them both to move back to California. Angad understood how close she was to her family, so he promised her that he would happily apply to jobs there after finishing school.

Another thing Kiara wanted to be transparent about was that she did not want to have any children. Growing up in such a big extended family with nieces and nephews, she saw how a lot of couples decided to have children because that was the cycle of life. During her childhood, Kiara lived in la-la land, dreaming about the perfect life of marriage and children because she was taught that a woman's role in life was to finish school, get married, produce babies, and dedicate their entire lives to their husband and children. Although she did not want to pass any judgment on those who were comfortable with this traditional lifestyle, motherhood was something Kiara was no longer interested in. Because she achieved independence, financial freedom, a career, and social life at a later age than most, she understood that being a mother would mean significantly adjusting the free-spirted lifestyle she created.

Kiara also believed that once a baby was born, a lot of couples started bickering over petty nonsense, kept a scorecard of which parent did more work for the child, and were always cranky with each other due to lack of sleep.

Although Kiara dearly loved her nieces, nephews, and babies in general, there were specific reasons why she chose not to have children.

1. She did not have the biological urge or maternal instincts.
2. Children did not fit into her free-spirited lifestyle.
3. She wanted to travel the world spontaneously.
4. Financially, it was not easy to raise a child.
5. She loved her sleep, so it would be hard waking up in the middle of the night.
6. Motherhood would require making too many adjustments in her career, time, and finances.
7. She did not have the energy!

8.  She did not want to physically go through the pain of childbirth.
9.  There was no guarantee that her child would take care of her in her old age.
10. Having a child also meant that the child's father would always be present in her life. So, even if, God forbid, they separated, he would never leave her life. Couples got divorced, but parents did not.

Angad had not been around children the way Kiara was, so he did not understand any of her concerns. Nevertheless, he still wanted to marry her and was supportive of her decision about not having children. She was impressed by his reaction because most men would not be as supportive. This was another big reason she thought he would be a great life partner.

Of course, they bickered occasionally but, it was nothing serious. In fact, most of the bickering they did was over how much she loved reality TV shows and how much he hated them. However, once while visiting Angad in San Francisco, an argument over something petty revealed a different side of Angad – a side Kiara had not witnessed before. A couple of his friends were waiting for them outside in the family room. By nature, Angad was extremely self-conscious and acutely aware about his image in front of others. Now that she was in his life, he also became self-conscious of how others perceived her. So, when Kiara raised her voice at him during that argument, he became furious, fearing his friends heard.

Glaring at her, he lowered his voice, pointed one finger, and repeatedly said, "Sit down right now. I am telling you to sit down and shut up right now. Do not show me your attitude. Sit . . . down . . . now." Kiara was very confused and taken aback because he never cursed or talked to her this way. Because she was shocked to see this strange side of him for the first time, she silently listened to him and sat down on the bed as he ordered. Following this, the room became so silent you could have heard a pin drop.

Shortly after, it was time for Kiara to catch her flight back to Sacramento. Angad was dropping her off at the airport. In the car ride, she was completely silent and had tears in her eyes the entire time. His anger had cooled off and he started apologizing to her. From the time he parked his car in the garage up until walking to the terminal, he repeatedly said, "Please, Kiara. I am so sorry. I did not mean to get mad at you like that. I am so sorry. Please do not leave me. I am so sorry." He repeatedly pleaded for her forgiveness.

Although Kiara was extremely hurt and shocked by his behavior, she appreciated how quickly he apologized. Kiara was overcome by Angad's emotional vulnerability; no other man had ever cried in her presence.

"As long as you promise to never speak with me like that again, I will forgive you," she said. He promised that he would never be so disrespectful towards her ever again. Of course, after seeing his tears and listening to his sincere apologies, she eventually forgave him, and they went back to their loving relationship again.

Angad and Kiara continued their long-distance relationship. For the rest of their courtship, he never ever spoke down to her again. On the contrary, he became even more loving and caring towards her. She believed his strange behavior was just a one-off situation where she must have provoked him to talk to her that way. After almost two years of dating, they got married in 2008.

# CHAPTER FOUR

# Small Fish in a Big Pond

*"Concrete jungle where dreams are made of. There's
nothing you can't do. Now you're in New York!"*

—Alicia Keys and Jay-Z

Angad was accepted by the Yale School of Law in New Haven, Connecticut. Kiara had a hard time with the idea of leaving her family and friends and moving to the East Coast. However, she was hopeful that they would move back to California once Angad graduated from Yale. Since she never lived outside of her hometown, Kiara chose to look at the move as an adventure and wanted to make the best of it.

Kiara and Angad decided to live in Stamford, Connecticut, because it was a neutral location between New Haven and New York City. Kiara had a good job in Sacramento and knew it would be a challenge interviewing for positions in the tri-state area from California. Kiara decided to resign from her job in Sacramento and start interviewing once they relocated to Connecticut. She did not want to move her car across the country since Angad was already taking his. Taking only one car was a practical decision, financially and logistically, but she lost a big part of her independence because she now had to rely on him to get around.

Within two weeks of relocating, Kiara landed a terrific job with an international media and marketing company in the Chrysler Building in midtown Manhattan. Navigating these major life changes—getting married, relocating, being away from friends and family, starting a new job—was challenging. She immediately took on the role of being a traditional wife where she cooked (which she hated), cleaned, and took care of the house all while working sixty hours per week.

Within the first month, she noticed a change in Angad. For some reason, he was not helping with the cooking, cleaning, laundry, or running errands. It was strange because when they were dating and she would visit him, he took care of all domestic duties and told her he loved cooking. He knew that Kiara did not like cooking and told her that they would share this task together once they got married.

By the second month of moving in with Angad, it was obvious to Kiara that he had become amazingly comfortable with her doing all the household chores. It was also around this time when she realized there was a huge disconnect between the Angad she dated for almost two years versus the one today. Anytime she pushed back on something, said no, or spoke up asking for his help, as Kiara could not do it all alone, it caused a lot of fights between them. As she got to know him better, she figured out that he had the typical mentality of a traditional Indian man where the wife was expected to do domestic duties on her own. Since he started studying at Yale Law School around this time, he could not work full-time, which meant Kiara was responsible for their finances in addition to domestic duties. Nevertheless, she wanted to be a supportive wife and looked forward to working in the city that never sleeps.

The corporate life in New York City was quite different from what she was used to in the suburbs of Sacramento. There, she felt like a big fish in a small pond, but in New York City, she felt quite the opposite. On the first day at work, she wore a low-cut, fitted black sleeveless dress that accentuated her curves. Kiara's new position was in a male dominated office with a bunch of bored and horny men. It seemed as if whenever she walked through the office that the room filled with sex fiends. However, as a newlywed, she was naïve and oblivious to their attention and flirtatiousness.

Her company's work culture was also ridiculously cutthroat where everyone cursed, screamed, and even threatened physical violence. It felt like Kiara was working with a bunch of low-ranking mobsters!

During her first week, she and her new colleagues went to happy hour in Columbus Circle where she met an attractive man named Joseph. Joe was a sales executive and worked for a hedge fund also located in The Chrysler Building. He was an Italian American and native New Yorker. Joe was 5ft 10 inches tall, had dark hair, a rugged stubble, athletic build, and spoke with a sexy Brooklyn accent. They started talking after he saw Kiara sitting near the bar area. He had an immediate crush on her right from the first moment they met and was easily infatuated by her beauty and sexiness.

Joe had a raunchy sense of humor which he enhanced by swearing like a sailor. There was an instant chemistry and palpable sexual tension between the two, but after she told him she was married, Joe was very respectful and content to remain friends. Because they worked in the same building, he and Kiara met up frequently after work.

Both worked late and were the last ones to leave their respective offices. Sometimes after work, they grabbed coffee together, hung out at Union Square Park, talked on the steps of the New York Library for hours, or walked around downtown. He treated her with great respect and kindness, and it really turned her on. Kiara would pleasure herself fantasizing about Joe when they were not together. It felt like love for him. Anytime things got stressful and lonely at home, Kiara talked to Joe because he was a fun distraction.

Angad concentrated only on school and could not give his full attention to her. Kiara was not a needy or clingy woman at all, so while he focused on school, she used her free time to explore beautiful New York City solo.

She did typical touristy things. For example, she:

- Took walks on the Brooklyn Bridge.
- Navigated the complex subway system.
- Drank frozen hot chocolate at Serendipity 3.
- Ate gourmet candy at Dylan's Candy Shop.
- Went running and bike riding around Central Park.
- Ate cupcakes at Magnolia Bakery.
- Ate at the yummiest Chinese restaurants and bakeries in Chinatown.
- Attended the San Gennaro Festival in Little Italy.
- Went on the *Sex and the City* bus tour.
- Watched the Radio City Rockettes - Christmas Spectacular show in Radio City Music Hall.
- Toured Rockefeller Center (Top of the Rock!), City Hall, and Bleecker Street, just to name a few.

Another thing she noticed about the city was that it was a mecca for meeting men. Everywhere she turned around, she was surrounded by the most gorgeous men she had ever seen—especially the rugged ones with the sexier Italian accents. She always had a thing for Italian men. Whether it was in her building, on the subway, crossing the street, in the coffee shops, or the park, it was exciting how much the city felt like it was raining men! She was like a kid in a candy shop where she was not allowed to touch anything and could only fantasize about having it all.

Kiara had to remind herself that she was married. Then again, just because she was married did not mean she could not be attracted to other men, right? She could look but not touch; playful flirtation was the closest she could come to the forbidden fruit.

On the flip side, Kiara received a lot of attention from many of the men. After seeing how vibrant and stimulating this city could be, she realized how sheltered her life had been up to this point. Kiara was creating so many amazing memories exploring the city alone or just hanging out with Joe. However, as soon as she got home, the reality and stresses of married life kicked in again.

# CHAPTER FIVE

# Caged Animal

"A house where a woman is unsafe is not a home."

—Amar Kumar Safi

Now a few months into relocating, the honeymoon phase of her marriage was noticeably over. Like many married couples, they argued over the house chores, bills, and lack of communication. However, the subject of Kiara's family sparked most of their big fights.

Angad suddenly became extremely jealous of how close she was to her family. He expected Kiara to prioritize him over her family, friends, career, and even herself. It annoyed him whenever she talked to family members on the phone. Sometimes she felt she had to speak softly or go to the bedroom and talk so that he would not hear. It bothered her that he was so jealous of her communication with them, but she still wanted to keep peace in the house. Kiara felt as if Angad wanted to isolate her from her family so that she would be fully dependent on him—and it irked the hell out of him whenever Kiara felt homesick.

Growing up, Angad never had that same bond with his own family; feeling emotionally neglected by them and getting cheated on by a former girlfriend left him extremely jealous and insecure. Anytime she was homesick, he sarcastically yelled at her, saying, "Why don't you go back to your family if you miss them so much?! Why are you even here with me? Go back to them!" His words hurt her feelings. She would think to herself, *Is this the same man who treated me like gold for two years?* Angad was notorious for apologizing quickly after he spoke rudely, expecting Kiara to accept the shallow apologies each time. One day, however, he surprised her with a honeymoon trip to Toronto, Canada. Angad had relatives in Toronto, so this was a great way for both to relax for a few days and get away.

Although he and Kiara had their usual verbal arguments, she noticed a strange change in him during this trip. One day Kiara and Angad were in the bedroom when Kiara became annoyed that her luggage zipper kept getting stuck, so she shouted and cursed at it in a fit. Angad was conscious of his goodie-two-shoes image and wanted his wife to be perceived the same way. He feared his relatives heard Kiara curse and became enraged by her yelling and cursing. To shut her down, he lost his temper and smacked her hard right on her back. Kiara was completely blindsided because he had never hit her before. This reminded her of the incident in San Francisco when they both argued in his room, but at that time, he did not hit her. It took only a few months of marriage for him to violently put his hands on her.

Kiara was completely shocked, frozen in place. She tried to rub her back to ease the pain. She stood there speechless and in pain, but instead of apologizing to Kiara, Angad immediately stormed out of the bedroom. After crying for ten minutes alone, she consoled herself, thinking that maybe she was just overreacting. She thought to herself, *I need to stop acting like a crybaby. It is not as if he hit me too hard. I need to just get over it. If I had not yelled at my stupid luggage the way I did, he would not slap me like that. Just get over it.* Thinking it was her fault, she pulled herself together, apologized to him for raising her voice, and things went back to normal again.

After a week traveling, they came back home to Connecticut. As days went by, he became extremely cranky and irritable about minor things, such as how badly she cooked, how terrible their neighborhood was, and how the house was not tidy enough. If he had a bad day in school, he took out his frustration on Kiara for no reason. Additionally, he was not satisfied with the geographical distance she had with her family, so he tried persuading her to move with him to Canada. "You know, the job market in Toronto is really great for your marketing field. We should pack our bags and move there someday," he told her. But Kiara genuinely had no interest relocating there. Moving away from family across country was hard enough, so moving out of country was not even an option in her mind. The less persuaded she was by him, the angrier he got. His irritability and the tension between them built up so badly that one day he banged the coffee table so hard it cracked.

In June 2010, just before her thirty-fifth birthday and after two years of marriage, a life altering incident happened between Kiara and Angad. This incident would psychologically scar her for life. Kiara and Angad were sitting on the bed talking, and she yelled at the remote control out of frustration because it was not working. Suddenly, he punched her left arm hard and said, "I do not like people yelling in front of me! Lower your voice! I have told you this many times! Do not me show your attitude! If you are so miserable being married to me, then go back to your family and stop yelling at the remote control!"

There was a painful tingling sensation in Kiara's arm followed by some numbness. She sat in pain listening to him yell and curse while she held her arm in shock because she could not believe he just punched her like that. Suddenly, out of nowhere, Angad went into a rage like a caged animal unexpectedly released. Angad jumped on top of Kiara, pinned her down on the bed, and began choking and punching her. He was so strong, athletic, and aggressive that half of her body fell off the bed, but he still would not stop choking, slapping, and punching her everywhere. Kiara was thrown around in every direction on that bed with him on top of her. This went on for ten minutes but was only the first round of beatings she got from him that day.

Once he was done with the attack, Angad left her on the bed and walked away to the kitchen. Looking like a complete mess, Kiara's hair was all over the place, and she laid there in a fetal position. She slowly gathered herself together and just sat frozen on the bed because she could not believe what he just done. This time, that painful sensation spread all over her body, followed by the strange numbness again. She could not even let out any tears because she was so shocked and numb. Kiara hoped this was a just one time beating and Angad would come back from the kitchen with an apology.

But she was wrong. Ten minutes later, Angad came back in the bedroom. Angad stared at her with wide eyes, and she noticed he was visibly shaking, his nostrils flared, and he was seething. That look in him scared her. After glaring for a few minutes in anger, he jumped on top of her again, pinned her down on the bed, and started hitting, slapping, and choking her once more. Because he was physically much stronger than she was, she just could not push him off. Anytime she tried pushing him off, he swung back hitting her even harder. After round two of the beatings was complete, he threw her back on the bed again and walked back to the kitchen once more. Once again, she just laid in a fetal position on the bed looking like a complete mess, staring out in space, heart beating amazingly fast.

The room was eerily silent, and Kiara believed her life depended on her staying silent. This time, she realized she was in big trouble. She was scared that the slightest noise from her would trigger another violent outburst. Kiara pulled herself together one more time, hoping that this second assault was the last. Out of fear, she slowly and very quietly walked over to the kitchen to see what he was doing. To her horror, she saw he was sitting on the floor staring downward and pointing a butcher knife at himself. She quietly walked away back to the bed again, hoping he did not see her behind him. She was terrified that he would hurt her or himself with that butcher knife. She was so petrified for her life that she wanted to run out of the house as fast she could. She feared, however that if he saw or heard her open the door, he would chase after her with that knife. Anything could happen. So instead, she tiptoed back to her bed and sat there, shaking, and silently praying.

Fifteen minutes later, Angad walked back to her again. This time, he held the butcher knife in his hand and stood there staring at her. Suddenly, he threw the knife on the floor, jumped on top of her again, pinned her down, and resumed slapping, punching, and strangling her. This third and final round of beating was the worst. He put all his weight on top of her, threw her around in every direction on the bed, and squeezed her throat hard while jamming her head to the bed's headboard.

This time, while screaming and cursing, he strangled her so tightly that she could not breathe at all. He held her head so aggressively against the bed's headboard that her neck twisted and could not move. The few seconds when she did try catching her breath, all she kept saying was, "Please do not kill me, Angad. My parents need me. I am begging you. I can't breathe. Please don't kill me. My parents need me." Her voice was hoarse from the continuous strangulation, so anytime she tried talking, she sounded like a robot. While baring his teeth and strangling her, all he kept screaming was, "You only care about your family! What about me?! You do not care about me at all! You only care about your family!"

As she kept begging and pleading for her life, she was completely at his mercy. As Kiara repeated the words, "My parents need me, please do not kill me," Angad became angrier. Her entire life flashed before her eyes. During those almost-final moments, the only images she saw were those of her with her mother and father.

Finally, she gasped, "I love you, Angad. Please don't kill me. I love you." After she said those words, he suddenly stopped strangling her. At that moment, Kiara did not feel any love, she said those three words solely to save her life. When he stopped, his whole face and body froze as he saw her lying on the bed in a vulnerable fetal position, recognizing the damage he had done. After realizing he was only minutes away from killing Kiara, Angad broke down and started bawling his eyes out.

"I am so sorry, Kiara. I cannot believe I just did this to you. I am so sorry. Please forgive me. I will never hit you again. It will never happen again," he said.

Despite being in physical pain, Kiara hugged and consoled him. Her heart broke watching him sob and in a twisted way she felt responsible for provoking him to cry and beat her. As she consoled him, she kept apologizing.

"I am so sorry. I provoked you. Please do not cry. I should not have behaved the way I did. This is all my fault. I provoked you to hit me," she responded.

However, Angad continued crying and apologizing to her the rest of the day. To show his remorse, he later went out and bought flowers, ice cream, and lunch for Kiara. He even held her head on his lap to comfort her as she fell asleep. By the end of that day, she felt like he was becoming his old sweet and loving self again, and she forgave him.

The next morning, Kiara had to get ready for work. She was still disturbed by the previous day's events. Looking in the mirror, she noticed the purple and blue bruises on her neck, shoulders, and arms and was horrified. She called Angad into the room to show him the bruises, but he scoffed, "Oh, c'mon, Kiara. You barely have any bruises. That is nothing. I did not hit you that hard where you would have a bruise. You are just being paranoid." She was annoyed at how he downplayed the bruises but decided to ignore it and get on with her day.

She composed herself and continued her normal routine as if nothing happened. Kiara was so preoccupied with covering up her injuries that she wore a short sleeve turtleneck with a light jacket despite it being a hot June day. She promised herself that she would never talk about this violent incident; it was going to be a secret she would take to her grave. In her heart, she thought Angad genuinely loved her and would follow through on his promise to never hurt her like that again.

During her commute to work, Kiara began having flashbacks from her childhood and young adult years up until yesterday when she was almost killed. She kept blaming the physical assault on herself, her insecurities, and decisions she had made. A few days later, Kiara decided to get back to her normal routine again, so she contacted Joe, and the two met up for coffee after work in Central Park. It was so nice to chat with him on the bench for a few hours and walk around the Park. Joe had such a magnetic personality and an adorable sense of humor that Kiara began to laugh again. Joe did not know about any of Kiara's marital issues and assumed her husband knew about the meetups with Kiara. He was an honest and respectable man, but Kiara kept this platonic friendship discreetly from her husband. That same evening, Angad called her.

"Hey, what time should I pick you up from the train station?" he asked.

"Um, 9 o'clock is fine," she said. Angad must have heard some hesitation in her voice.

"Are you alone?" he asked.

After a brief pause, she answered, "Yes."

Because that violent incident was such a huge turning point for her emotionally and psychologically, she started losing interest and respect in her marriage. She felt bad lying to Angad about being alone, but since the wounds were so fresh in her mind and on her body, she quickly let go of the guilt.

The next weekend Kiara and Angad flew to Sacramento to celebrate her thirty-fifth birthday with her family. By that time, her bruises had faded so she felt more comfortable seeing them. She felt so ashamed of the situation, which enforced her determination to keep the incident a secret. A big part of her wanted to protect Angad because if she told her family the truth, they would hate him and pressure her to leave him. And besides, he promised that it would never happen again.

While part of her felt eerie seeing her whole family so soon after that incident, the other part felt as if nothing happened at all. Around her friends and family members, Angad naturally became the sweet and loving person they knew him to be. Nobody would ever guess that this was the same man who had choked her ten days earlier. She was so confused by how he could switch from violent and angry to sweet and charming so quickly; it was a classic case of Dr. Jekyll and Mr. Hyde.

By the time they returned to Connecticut, their relationship improved significantly, and Kiara felt they had gotten past the rough patch. For many months, he did not yell at her or put his hands on her again, and they were back in the honeymoon phase. Although she did not respect him like before, the thought of divorcing him did not cross her mind. She thought to herself, *Every woman must compromise to make her marriage work. I do not want to break my marriage up over this. All married couples fight, so I will need to compromise and just get over it.*

Angad graduated from law school in 2011 and was hired by a law firm in Atlanta, Georgia. This was one of the jobs Kiara so painstakingly helped him prepare for. The pay was not that great, but Angad saw this as a major step in his legal career. Since Kiara knew this move to Atlanta was only for the interim, she did not want to relocate there, and there was no point in staying alone in Connecticut. Instead, she moved back to her family home in Sacramento and got a new job there. Surprisingly, Angad was supportive of this decision. Kiara used this opportunity to distance herself from him.

# CHAPTER SIX

# It will Never Happen Again

"When violence against women is no longer societally
accepted, no longer kept a secret; when everyone
understands that even one case is too many.
That's when it will change."

**—Joe Biden**

From 2011 to 2015, Kiara and Angad had settled into a long-distance marriage. The perks of a long-distance marriage were that both had their own respective spaces to concentrate on their careers, and Kiara felt safe again with her family and friends in her hometown. Both met up every couple of weeks. Kiara received a lot of flak from people in her hometown about her long-distance marriage. She constantly heard things such as, "Couples are supposed to live together in the same house," or, "He will cheat on you since you left him there alone." Sadly, nobody knew the truth about the violence she went through, so she did her to best to ignore the criticisms.

In 2016, Angad got a better-paying job in Portsmouth, New Hampshire. After relocating there, his attitude towards her and their marriage changed. After over four years of a long-distance marriage, he now expected Kiara to relocate to New Hampshire with him. She did not want to join him because she was much happier living in her hometown and had a great-paying job, so she pushed back.

"I already relocated once for you. I have had to leave and find a new job a few times already, which has caused a lot of setbacks in my career," she explained to him.

"I don't care. You are my wife, and you need to live wherever I live," Angad replied.

Angad's usual tactic was that anytime he wanted her to do something for him was to become extra affectionate. Angad knew that Kiara would not leave her family and relocate with him again if he behaved badly with her. So now, he became sweet and loving again.

"Please, Kiara, I really miss you. We have not lived together for so many years. I want us to start living together again. I promise if you move back with me, we will have such an exciting time exploring New Hampshire together," he told her.

During the years they lived apart Angad mellowed significantly. He was proving himself to be the good person she knew him to be when they first met, so she was finally open to the idea of moving in with him again. Once again, she left another good job in Sacramento, found a new one in New Hampshire, and relocated across country, leaving her friends and family behind. Kiara had decided to give their relationship another chance.

They settled into an upper-class neighborhood in a town near Portsmouth. After moving in together, they both did the typical touristy things around New England, such as:

- Touring the homes of Paul Revere and John Paul Jones.
- Going on a fall foliage tour.
- Going on Harbor cruise rides.
- Spending Christmas in Portsmouth, New Hampshire, and Boston, Massachusetts.

Kiara landed a great job with a healthcare technology marketing company downtown. While Angad got to work from home, her commute was one hour each way, without traffic. Kiara resumed the role of being a traditional wife where cooking, cleaning, and running errands were her responsibility in addition to working a full-time job. Within a few months of living together, Kiara sensed the honeymoon phase ending. Once again, she became a scapegoat anytime Angad had a bad day at work. He faced a lot of racial discrimination at work and felt his junior white co-workers were given more respect than him. Instead of fighting back at work like he should have, he took out his frustration on Kiara and used her as his verbal punching bag.

Another thing that still bothered him was how involved Kiara was with her family. She had always pitched in towards her share of the family's responsibilities ever since her first job as a teenager. However, he now expected her to drop those responsibilities and help pay off his student loan. In addition, he became jealous of her tight bond with her family again. Anytime she talked to them on the phone, she had to go the bedroom and close the door because he hated their calls; simply hearing her laugh with them got on his nerves. As usual, he expected her to focus her time, energy, and money towards him only because that was what a good wife is supposed to do.

Kiara also became resentful of how the burden of cooking and cleaning was solely on her shoulders all over again. She did not have the luxury of working from home the way he did, so it was very unfair to do all those chores by herself without his help. These things reminded her of their Connecticut days. After over five years, he had not changed the way she thought he would. To avoid dealing with him, she spent more time in the office, which made him even angrier because she would be too exhausted to prepare dinner for him. The situation soon went from bad to worse.

One Saturday morning in July of 2017, Angad and Kiara got into an argument, which intensified very quickly. Out of nowhere, Angad threw the plate of food she prepared for him towards her.

Luckily, she moved quickly before the plate could hit her. Fearing his temper would escalate, she immediately went up to him and started apologizing for provoking this argument. He was so fired up that he did not want to be around her. Somewhere in the back of his mind, he knew that if he did not physically leave the apartment at that moment, something bad would happen. So, as he went to grab his shoes, Kiara followed him around repeatedly apologizing and begging him not to be angry with her. Fed up, Angad turned around towards her in extreme rage, grabbed her throat with both hands, threw her against the wall, and began choking her.

Grinding his teeth, he seethed, "I told you already that I do not like people shouting. Don't you ever talk to me like that again, do you understand that?!"

Cornered against the wall, she could not move, breathe, or talk, and just like the last time, her voice was hoarse from the strangulation. Then, he dragged Kiara by her throat to the bedroom, threw her on the bed, and pinned her down. He twisted both of her arms then hit her with all his might in the middle of her back. That slap felt like a thousand pins and needles stabbing her whole body as she shook in sharp pain. The pain was so unbearable that she rolled over on her back to try and ease it. He pinned her down again, punched both arms, slapped her ear, and resumed the strangling. Once more, she saw her life flash before her eyes as she struggled to breathe.

After Angad was done, he threw her on the bed, stormed out of the room, grabbed his keys, and left the house. Kiara pulled herself together and slowly walked over to the bathroom mirror. When she saw her reflection, she was absolutely horrified. There were dark pink lines and patches on both arms, reddened ears, pink bruises on her throat from the strangulation, and a large imprint of his hand that branded her back. Seeing the injuries on her body, she was so ashamed of making eye contact with herself in the mirror. She broke down and completely bawled her eyes out. Once again, she thought to herself, *How did I reach this point in my life? How stupid can I be for getting another beating from a man who says he loves me?*

She had a déjà vu moment from when he previously assaulted her like this in Connecticut. Back then, he had promised never to hit her again. This time, she did something different. She took photos of her bruises and emailed them to herself to save the evidence. An hour later, Angad came home, walked up to her, and began crying. He affectionately held her in his arms and repeatedly apologized.

"This is not right. I cannot believe I did this to you again, Kiara. I am so sorry. I promise I will never hit you again. It will never happen again."

After hearing him apologize repeatedly and bawl like a baby, her anger faded away, and she began sympathizing with him. She consoled him.

"No, please do not say sorry. This was completely my fault. I should not have behaved that way. I am so sorry for provoking you. This was my fault. I deserved it," she replied. The rest of that day he became loving, sweet, and caring again.

Within the next few days, things were slowly going back to normal again. However, when the dust settled, she had a stern conversation with him.

"If you ever touch me like that again, I will leave you. This is the second time I am forgiving you, but if you hit me again, I will leave you forever," she told him sternly.

However, instead of apologizing and reiterating that he would never do it again, he said, "You know what, I think we should just separate. I know I made a big mistake by hitting you, but you provoked me. I kept telling you repeatedly not to follow me when I was grabbing my shoes to leave, but you provoked me to hit you and then you act like the victim. Look what you made me do."

She started believing him that maybe she caused the beating. This was the point in their relationship when she began feeling physically scared of being around him.

After a few weeks, there were two separate incidents where he pushed her against a wall violently. From then on, whenever Kiara noticed Angad's anger escalating, she would quickly grab her purse, run out the house, and stay in her car out of fear. She did not know what do to or where to go. After staying away from him for hours, she would eventually go back home, apologize to him, and all would be normal again.

# CHAPTER SEVEN

# Loss of Power

"Relationships with narcissists are held in place
by hope of a 'someday better,' with little evidence
to support it will ever arrive."

**–Dr. Ramini Durvasula**

I n late 2017, Angad accepted a lucrative job offer to lead a top law
firm in Austin, Texas. It was another one of the jobs Kiara helped
him prepare for. Although she was genuinely happy for his big career
opportunity, she had lost love, interest, and respect for him by this
point. After relocating twice already, she did not want to relocate for
him a third time. Again, Kiara used this opportunity as an excuse to
move back with her family in Sacramento. Discreetly, she interviewed
with a new company in Sacramento and accepted a job offer. When
Angad heard about this, he was enraged that she was planning to move
back with her parents again.

"If you don't want to move with me to Texas, I prefer you stay
here in New Hampshire rather than moving back with your family,"
he told her.

"But I don't want to live in New Hampshire by myself. I moved
here for you, and now that you are moving again, where does this

leave me? I can't keep moving from state to state and switch jobs repeatedly," she responded.

"You are my wife, and you have to follow wherever I go," he sternly told her.

"Truth is you don't really care where I live as long as I don't live with my parents. I don't understand why you want to isolate me from them," she replied.

After arguing over this topic for weeks, Kiara continued with this new job offer and started planning moving back to Sacramento.

In January 2018, Kiara helped Angad pack, relocate, and went with him to Texas to help him get settled. Shortly after they arrived, she sensed his constant irritation and anger growing. Angad was still extremely furious that she was moving back to California instead of with him.

Once while shopping at Target, Kiara took a call from a family member and Angad's blood started to boil over. As usual, he expected her to ignore her family and only focus on him. Later that night as they were unpacking, Kiara sat on the floor struggling to set up the Wi-Fi. She was not as tech-savvy as Angad, so out of frustration, he was screaming and cursing at her because she could not set it up correctly. While she continued to struggle, Angad smashed the boxes on the kitchen floor in anger, ran over to Kiara and slapped her hard on the back.

"Listen, you fatso! Look, this is what you are supposed to do with the modem!" he screamed. Kiara just sat there in silence, placing one hand on her back. She could not believe he had hit her again.

"What?! Oh, what are you going to do now, act like a victim again?!" he screamed.

"You hit me," she said.

"I did NOT hit you! I only tapped you, you bitch! Stop acting like a victim! You always provoke my anger and then act like a victim to gain sympathy!" Then he stormed out of the room.

The eerie silence petrified Kiara as she worried about what he would do next. She wanted to run out of the house but worried he would chase her. After ten minutes of silence, Angad threw his car keys at her and screamed.

"Here, take the keys, go back to the hotel! Go back to your family, you bitch!" he shouted. Luckily, Kiara moved before the keys could hit her.

She quickly gathered her bags and went back to the hotel. She needed to move away from him as soon as possible. After a few hours when his anger cooled off, he came back to their hotel room and without a word got into bed and went to sleep next to her.

The next morning Kiara packed in preparation for her flight back to New Hampshire. As she got ready for the airport and was leaving the hotel room, Angad woke up and tried stopping her.

"Your flight is not until three hours. Why are you leaving so early?" he asked.

"Because I do not want to stay with you anymore. The last time you beat me, I told you that if you ever touch me like that again, I will leave you," she firmly reminded him.

"I did NOT hit you, I only tapped you. Why are you acting like a victim again?" he argued as he tried stopping her at the door.

"Do not touch me or I will scream and everyone in the hotel will hear me. I should have left you a long time ago," she angrily said.

Fearing the hotel neighbors would hear her scream, he finally let her go. Kiara quickly got an Uber and left for the airport. She cried the entire trip back to New Hampshire, realizing that she could not continue being with a man who constantly put his hands on her and insulted her. Immediately after that, she relocated from New Hampshire to Sacramento, moved back with her parents, and started a new job all over again.

After a few weeks of living long-distance again, Angad began missing her. She was still terribly upset with him and kept ignoring his calls and text messages. In her mind, she had no interest in keeping him in her life. Then one day, Angad surprised her with a luxury suitcase delivered to her house as another way of apologizing. Seeing this expensive gift from him, she was pleasantly surprised that he spent this amount of money on her. Then she began questioning herself: *Did I make a mistake by leaving him again? If we do get a divorce, will I regret this decision later in life? All marriages are complicated, and every married couple fights. But what if five or ten years from now I look back with regret that I did not try harder to save my marriage?* Once again, her heart melted, she forgave him, and she told Angad that she would move back in with him again.

Luckily, Kiara received approval from her new job in Sacramento to work remotely from Texas, so she moved in with Angad in February 2018. Kiara was hopeful about the move, but little did she know, she was in for another rude awakening.

Once she reached Texas, Angad picked her up from the airport, and things in their relationship were going perfect. But after a few days, Angad began asserting his power over her in various ways as his attitude again went from bad to worse. For instance, Kiara was not allowed to put her clothes in the big walk-in closet. Instead, she had to use the hallway linen closet. That closet was in a dark corner, so she had to use her phone's flashlight to look for her belongings. To say that the cleaning and cooking was her responsibility was an understatement and he continued to insult whatever she cooked. In addition, when he came home after work, he would walk past her without even looking at her. The only time he talked to her was when he wanted something from her, otherwise he was cold and deliberately ignored her. If she parked his car incorrectly, if he had a bad day at work, or if Uber Eats messed up his food delivery order, he took out his frustration on Kiara, saying, "Go back to your family. Why are you even here? You have no interest in this relationship! Just go back. I do not even want you here, bitch."

After having sex with her, he would say, "Don't think this is going to change anything!"

Furthermore, he firmly told Kiara that he would never visit her family in Sacramento ever again. He expected his wife to follow him wherever he decided to move for his career, he did not care to reciprocate, and he would not join her if she asked him to visit her parents.

"I hate your mother and father. They are beggars; they have ruined my life! Every single problem in my life is caused by your parents!" he shouted. Kiara was genuinely confused why he kept blaming her parents for no reason. Angad and Kiara had met on their own, dated for a couple of years, and made the decision to marry without family pressures. Kiara's parents always treated Angad like their own son and supported his relationship with their daughter right from the very beginning. Yes, she was awfully close with her parents but to blame them for everything was completely unjustified and absurd.

Kiara's family members tried contacting Angad to fix any potential misunderstandings, but he never responded. He even declined multiple calls from her mother and told Kiara, "Tell your mother to never call me again!" Angad's biggest complaint was that they were too loving towards their daughter and let her stay in their house while they lived apart. He expected them to kick her out of their house.

She still ignored his criticisms and insults towards her family, hoping that his anger was temporary. A few months later, Kiara's niece was graduating from college; Kiara begged Angad to attend the ceremony with her.

"Please, Angad, will you come with me? I am going to feel so ashamed in front of all my family members. Please do not put me in this embarrassing position where I do not know how to answer when they ask why you are not there," she begged and pleaded.

He callously replied, "I do not care. I will never visit your family again. I just don't care."

Not only did Angad cold-heartedly refuse to fulfill this wish for Kiara, but he kept pressuring her to quit her Sacramento job and look for something new in Austin. She felt lucky to have found a company that allowed her to work remotely, but he still was not satisfied. He wanted her to detach herself from Sacramento not only personally but professionally.

Even after researching companies in Austin, she told him, "I do not have any good career prospects here."

He replied, "That's your problem, not mine."

To move on, Kiara would suggest the two go out sightseeing and tour the beautiful city of Austin. However, Angad had no interest in taking her out socially and kept making excuses about being too busy with work. Despite feeling low, Kiara tried to make the best of her marital situation and explored the city of Austin by herself. Just like her New York City days where she explored the area on her own, she decided to do the same thing while living in Austin. So, she did the typical touristy things, such as:

- Going running downtown every evening after work
- Touring the Bullock Texas History Museum
- Attending the Austin City Limits Music Festival
- Taking a road trip to San Antonio to attend a three-day yoga and wellness retreat.

With regards to the retreat, Kiara begged Angad to join her and make it a weekend getaway. As usual, he was not interested, so she made the trip alone.

Four months later in May 2018, Angad's treatment of Kiara did not improve. Since she worked from home all the time, she did not interact with her co-workers in person. Not having any friends, family, or co-workers to interact with was tough enough, but living with a husband who treated her like she was invisible became unbearable. Kiara started feeling like her only purpose of being there was to cook, clean, and let him have sex with her. Basically, she felt like she was his bitch. Feeling so abandoned and disrespected, she fell into a depression and cried herself to sleep every night. As a woman who was usually polished and refined, she lost motivation to dress up, put on makeup, or comb her hair. Feeling like a mess physically, psychologically, and emotionally, she kept thinking to herself, *Why am I here?*

Because she was determined to make this relationship work, she avoided any conflicts with Angad and did not engage in any arguments. Her voice completely softened up around him, and she listened to everything he told her to do just to keep the peace at home. Finally, she now became the obedient and disciplined wife Angad always expected her to be. What Kiara did not realize was that, while attempting to make this relationship work, she started sacrificing each of her strengths. One by one, she lost her courage, self-esteem, self-dignity, sense of humor, independence, outspokenness, and the ability to say no. The inner power that she worked to gain her entire life, she lost.

Now, she became that timid and fragile little girl from her childhood who was too scared to fight the bullies who physically and emotionally abused her in school; the one who did not have courage to fight the group of mean girls who told her she had no worth; the one who was too scared to fight back the kids who stole her food and lunch money, threw pencils at her, and made her cry daily. Many times, she wanted to call her family and tell them the truth about how her husband was treating her. But just like the little girl in her childhood who thought tattle-telling was wrong, she could not bring herself to tell her family what was going on.

One evening, Angad got into a big verbal fight with Kiara, which went on for five hours. Fed up with his treatment of her, she started defending herself to him. During that fight, Angad compared her to a dog, a servant, kept cursing about her aging mother and father, and called her vulgar curse words in Hindi such *"madarchod"* (motherfucker), *"bhenchod"* (sisterfucker), and *"chutiya"* (cunt). He then went on to insult her status and the status of her parents.

*"Teri aukad hi kya hai? Apni aukat me raho. Tum apni aukat se upar baat kar rahi ho. Are, tere maa baap ki aukat hi kya?"* he shouted. (What is your worth and your mother and father's value? You better stay in your lane and only talk on your level).

As usual, when she saw his temper escalate, she shut her mouth and quickly sat down on the sofa away from him. After five hours of verbally attacking her, Angad sat down and played his video games while Kiara sat on the other chair crying her eyes out. He had no remorse, and instead he laughingly ignored her. After quietly staring at him for thirty minutes as he played his video games, something triggered her. She realized that his mistreatment of her was not a temporary phase. He only wanted an obedient and submissive wife to push around and had no intention of loving or respecting her.

After years of tolerating, ignoring, and forgiving his bad behavior, she thought to herself, *Enough is enough.* Kiara quietly walked into the bedroom, locked the door, booked the first flight out to Sacramento, and packed all her luggage.

An hour later when Angad saw her luggage packed, he quickly transformed and became sweet, loving, and apologetic all over again. Suddenly, he began pleading with her to stay and promised to take her to Dallas and other exciting places if she stayed.

"Please do not go. I am sorry for fighting with you again. Stay here with me, and I promise I will take you to Dallas next week. Please just let this stupid fight go," he begged.

"No, I will not stay here any longer. I am leaving first in the morning," she said before going to sleep.

Ironically, the four months she lived there, he never once wanted to go anywhere with her, but now that she was leaving, he suddenly had the desire to take her on a trip. In the back of his mind, Angad did not believe Kiara would follow through on leaving, since she had come back so many times before.

Her flight was at 5:00 a.m. Angad woke up just as Kiara was getting ready to leave for the airport. Now, he sensed this was different and that Kiara was serious. As she walked towards the door, he tried stopping her.

"I thought we decided you were not going to go?" he rhetorically asked in a stern tone.

"No, **you** decided I was not going to go. I told you already last night that I am leaving first thing in the morning, but you did not believe me," she responded. Kiara was in tears, feeling like a complete failure that she could not save her marriage, and still, she firmly held on to her luggage, opened the door, and **she left.**

# CHAPTER EIGHT

# Method of Healing

"You survived the abuse.
You are going to survive the recovery."

—Mariska Hargitay

A week after leaving Angad, Kiara was in a confused state of mind and did not know where her life was headed. It felt like she was spinning through a revolving door and she was scared about her future. She started feeling unsure again of whether she made the right decision or not by leaving him. Although she did not feel any affection towards her marriage, she also did not want to go through the process of divorce again.

By this point, her friends and family were so concerned about Kiara's mental health that they strongly recommended she see a therapist. She was resistant to seeing one not because of the social stigma attached to it, but because she genuinely did not think she needed it. She thought to herself, *Just because I am having marital issues does not mean I need professional help. I can handle this.* She also felt like it would be a waste of time and money to talk to someone about her dilemmas. *This is only a rough patch. I can handle this.* What Kiara did not realize was that she was suffering from PTSD

(Post Traumatic Stress Disorder). Her symptoms had become second nature and she did not even notice them.

Her loved ones explained that therapists were professionally trained in observing and treating human behaviors. They identified negative patterns and cycles that she might not see in herself. When talking to friends and family about her problems, they would always have some subjective biases because they loved and cared about her. On the contrary, a therapist did not know their patients on a personal level, nor did they know the individuals the patients were talking about; therefore, their feedback was completely objective and unbiased. After a lot of persuasion, Kiara decided to seek professional help and made that first appointment in June 2018.

Kiara was matched with a therapist named Diane who had extensive experience treating people who suffered from PTSD. Her patients included war veterans, victims of abuse, and domestic violence. Initially, Kiara was very guarded in her sessions with Diane.

"I came to see you because my family kept encouraging me. I'm not sure therapy will help me but, I'm going through some confusion about my marriage," said Kiara.

"So, tell me about your marriage and what you feel the issues are" said Diane. Kiara talked about how she met Angad, how long they have been married, the fights they had had, etc.

"When you talk about the fights in your marriage, was it verbal or more?" Diane bluntly asked.

"Well, yes, he did get physical with me a few times, but that was only because I caused those fights. I am not an easy woman to live with, I provoked his anger. By nature, he is a very gentle man and would not hurt a fly," Kiara replied.

"A gentle man does not physically abuse anyone, especially his wife," Diane said.

"Abuse? I do not think my marriage would be considered abusive. Yes, things were physically violent at times, but I would not label him as an abusive husband. I am a strong, educated, affluent woman, and I can handle this," Kiara argued.

"Abuse happens on all socio-economic levels. It is a common misconception that these things only occur in homes of lower socioeconomic status. I have treated victims of abuse who were physicians, lawyers, politicians, and successful entrepreneurs, and some of their abusers were highly educated and successful." explained Diane.

Kiara was beginning to get frustrated. "Look, I am nobody's victim. All couples fight and have rough patches. I start fights also. If I had not behaved the way I did, he never would have put his hands on me. And besides, it is not like he beat me all the time," she replied.

"What your husband did is something called intimate partner violence or domestic violence. Nothing you did caused him to hit you. Abuse is all about power and control and can be in the form of physical, emotional, psychological, and even financial," said Diane. "Are you familiar with the term narcissist?"

"I have heard of it, but I don't think I personally know anyone who is narcissistic," Kiara replied.

"I believe you do. You are married to one. Your husband has the typical traits of something called Narcissistic Personality Disorder (NPD). Narcissists have a long-term pattern of exaggerated feelings of self-importance, an excessive craving for admiration, and struggle with empathy. Narcissists do not care about anyone but themselves. Even when they seem nice and caring, they are putting on a show until they get what they want," Diane explained.

"Angad was not angry and mean all the time. He does have a good side," Kiara said.

"Even serial killers have a good side to them. There is something called positive reinforcement, which means a person gets rewarded for listening to someone and doing what they are told. For example, anytime you did what your husband expected of you, he immediately became nice as a way of rewarding you. Then after the dust settled, he expected you to continue doing those things, so eventually he stopped rewarding you; and that is when you would end up seeing the ugly side of his personality," said Diane.

"I thought he just had anger issues. So, if he is considered abusive, how did he become this way suddenly?" Kiara asked innocently.

"Abusers do not suddenly become abusive out of nowhere. It is something they learned from their childhood. Whether they were physically abused themselves or they have witnessed abusive relationships, they think this behavior of having power and control over someone else, especially a significant other, is normal," Diane explained.

"He was never physically abused by anyone at home. He had a very loving relationship with his parents, and they had a strong marriage. But he lived in a joint family where he saw his uncle beat his aunt on a regular basis. Then he witnessed his aunt burn herself to death," responded Kiara.

Diane gasped.

The first few sessions were a big challenge for Diane because Kiara blatantly refused to accept that her marriage was abusive and that her husband was an abuser. In fact, she refused to even use the word "abuse." Growing up in such a protected and loving household, she was never exposed to this subject. Her parents had a loving relationship, so she was completely ignorant to the traits of an abusive husband.

In addition to learning about Kiara's marital issues, Diane also asked her to describe challenges and insecurities from her childhood. After learning about how Kiara had been bullied by other children, Diane explained how that treatment was also a form of emotional abuse. Emotional abuse did not just happen in intimate relationships. When people told her she had no worth, was unwanted, repeatedly made her cry, told her to die, and insulted her every day, she grew up believing their opinions. When they told her that she was not good enough, she believed them, and that was exactly why she grew up insecure and constantly fighting off inner demons. On top of everything, culture and society taught her that girls were supposed to be sweet and gentle, that was how Kiara behaved, and bullies took advantage of her behavior.

"Bullies pick on people who are pickable," Diane explained.

Diane realized that Kiara still had many suppressed issues from her school days. As Diane got to know Kiara better, she connected all the dots in Kiara's life. Diane learned that Kiara had been dealing with difficult people from childhood, young adult years, and into her marriage that had gone on unaddressed. It was time to fight all those inner demons and finally let go.

After three therapy sessions, Diane decided to try something different. She changed her technique by using Eye Movement Desensitization and Reprocessing (EMDR) an interactive psychotherapy technique used to relieve psychological stress. Diane explained that EMDR was initially used to treat war veterans who were suffering from PTSD but, it was such an effective tool that therapists were now using EMDR to treat persons who suffered from any type of trauma.

Diane explained that "EMDR is a mental time-travel strategy where you can process any traumatic memories. I have used this technique to help treat many forms of PTSD as well as victims of abuse. We cannot go back into time and change anything. But through EMDR, we can try to desensitize you from those memories, so that you are more detached from them emotionally."

On the beginning of their fourth therapy session together, Diane instructed Kiara on how they would proceed with the therapy. Diane stated that she would be moving two fingers in front of her vision and as Kiara tracked the movement, Diane would guide her through her trauma. And then, Diane began asking her some tough questions.

"Think about the first incident when your husband beat you. Can you describe to me in graphic detail where you were and what exactly happened?" she asked.

In a softened and slow tone, Kiara described the first incident when her husband physically assaulted her, including the strangulation. As she continued the descriptions, tears flowed down her face, and she got choked up. The more choked up she was, the more Diane proceeded in asking tougher questions while continuously moving two fingers across Kiara's line of vision.

When Kiara stopped talking, Diane asked, "How does this experience make you really feel today? What would you say to that woman who just got this beating from her husband? Did she ask him to her hurt her?"

"I feel angry. I feel enraged and appalled. I am beyond furious. How dare he hit me?! How dare he choke me?! I get angry with people, but have I ever beat anyone? It was not my fault that he abused me. I never asked to get a beating. How dare he?! He is just an abusive narcissistic son of a bitch!" Kiara shouted as she cried.

Diane was happy to see that Kiara finally used the word abuse since she previously refused to accept that her marriage was abusive. Then Diane asked Kiara to think back to the bullying from her childhood and the times she lost the desire to live.

"What would you say to that little girl?" Diane asked.

"I would tell her that, 'You need to go tell your teachers, parents, and your sisters about those bullies and what they all did to you. Don't believe them when they say you have no worth because you are perfect, and they are only picking on you because they have no guts to go head-to-head with people who they think are stronger than them.' I also want to say, 'I'm sorry you could not defend yourself, and I am sorry for your bad experiences. But you have a bright future ahead, and you will be proud of the woman you grow up to be. You are a survivor of adversities. You are a warrior, and I am so proud of how you ferociously protected yourself. You are a survivor." Kiara continued shouting and crying.

"You know what I just heard right now as you spoke to that little girl? I heard your love and protection for her. You really love her with all your heart," Diane responded.

While Kiara initially approached her sessions with rigid formality and composure, she reached a breaking point during this visit, but she also had a breakthrough. This session was so enlightening and intense that she screamed, cursed, and bawled her eyes out for over an hour. Prior to this session, she genuinely did not realize how poisonous her bottled-up emotions had been for decades. By nature, Kiara was someone who did not like to cry in front of others because she did not want to be perceived as fragile or weak. On that day, Kiara understood that showing vulnerability was a sign of strength, not weakness.

Kiara had been called a victim by Angad on a regular basis for so long that anytime she felt like crying, she told herself to just get over it. Now crying in front Diane, Kiara released the heavy burden of tears she had been carrying in her heart for so long. Breaking down her composure was exactly what her mind, body, and soul needed. This was a big turning point when Kiara finally admitted to herself that her husband was abusive, narcissistic, and controlling.

Another important aspect of EMDR was consciously thinking about a happy place. Diane asked Kiara to think about a place that made her feel the most brave and powerful. It did not have to be a real place and could be fictitious.

"For some reason, I see myself standing on stage giving a motivational speech. Whether it is at a TED Talk or something equivalent to it, my mind always dreams about standing on stage speaking to audience members and the media about my personal journey and resilience."

"So, think about standing on that stage. What are you wearing?" asked Diane.

"A stunning dark purple business casual dress and black high heels," answered Kiara.

"Who all do you see sitting in the audience listening to you?" asked Diane.

"I see my immediate family, extended family members, and closest friends all happy for me. I see people from school, the mean girls who always left me out and the guys who always pushed me around. I see the people who have relentlessly rejected me my entire life. I see people from different workplaces. I see little girls and young women in my audience, and I can tell they are looking at me as a source of inspiration. I see the person who never respected or believed in me, my husband. I see all individuals who have always loved me and those who did not care about me" Kiara said as she continued to bawl her eyes out.

"How does it feel standing on that stage? I want you to go deep inside your heart, bring out that emotion, and really feel it," said Diane.

"I feel courageous and strong speaking so eloquently about my personal journey. I feel powerful being recognized as a source of inspiration to the many little girls and young women who doubt themselves. For the first time in my life, I feel respected standing on that stage, and it is such an amazing feeling," Kiara continued.

By the end of that fourth session, she finally felt this wonderful sense of self-realization as she recognized that all these years, she was in an abusive marriage. Diane's professional training and her objective viewpoint allowed Kiara to admit this to herself. Diane also explained that EMDR was intense and influential on the mind so it should only be done with a trained professional who was licensed to perform that type of therapy. Due to the effectiveness of EMDR, Diane chose to continue this technique for all of Kiara's sessions moving forward.

As Kiara continued her therapy sessions, she realized it was one of the healthiest choicest she had made in a long time.

Her doctor's tough love encouraged Kiara's decision to not relocate to Texas with Angad. Accepting the job offer from the company in Sacramento was a good opportunity to leave the relationship. After relocating twice already, she did not want to do it again for a man who had no respect for her. Moving back to her mother and father's home was a haven. So late 2017, she did something very brave; she called her immediate family and told them Angad beat her on two separate incidents. Her family was supportive of her decision to move back. When they told her, "Please, come home," she suddenly felt a ray of hope.

In January 2018, both Kiara and Angad had relocated to their respective new cities and jobs and had a long-distance marriage again. Unfortunately, stage four is the toughest phase for most victims to sustain because once they leave, they charmingly get pulled back in again by their abusers. In the past, Kiara had not been an exception.

*note to my readers:*

*The stories shared in this book are not intended to fully describe specific medical treatments nor are they meant as recommendations. Please refer to appropriate medical professionals for information and treatment.*

# CHAPTER NINE

# *Sacred Awakening*

"We don't laugh at the same joke again,
why do we cry on the same problem again?"

—Gaur Gopal Das

The more Kiara continued her therapy sessions and educated herself about intimate partner violence, the more it was all starting to make sense to her. As much as she wanted to permanently leave this marriage, there was also a part of her that was afraid of going through the process of another divorce, of being alone and restarting her life all over again. Kiara was at a fork in the road, and she could not decide whether to stay or leave her marriage.

Diane advised her that she needed a change of scenery to give her mind a rest, and that a trip out of town would be healthy. Kiara had completely forgotten how much she loved traveling and decided to plan a trip and take a serious break, clear her mind, and focus on herself.

With so much confusion all around her, she needed desperately to do some soul searching and wanted to start a brand-new spiritual journey just as Julia Roberts' character did in the movie, *Eat Pray Love.* --Where should she start and what exactly should she do? It was important for her to find deeper meaning in her everyday existence. There were many beautiful countries in Asia that she had always wanted to visit, but the place she thought would provide her the most peace right now was her motherland, —India. Kiara had relatives there, but she was in a bad rut and felt so out of sync with her life that she wanted to experience a new place in India. The idea of traveling solo and nourishing her soul felt scary, but also exciting.

Kiara booked a ten-day vacation to Goa, India. Goa is a coastal state located in Southwest India surrounded by the beautiful Arabian Sea. Goa was a Portuguese territory for centuries and still has a lot of the country's cultural influences today. Socially, it is known to have some of the world's best spiritual retreats and is also, a big beach party destination. Kiara always wanted to visit Goa and had not had the opportunity until now. After extensive research, she booked accommodations in Mapusa, a city in North Goa, for a luxurious, mindful, reset and renew wellness retreat. One week later, Kiara boarded her flight to Goa.

Emotionally, her energy was still low. The passenger seated next to Kiara, an elderly Caucasian woman, seemed to sense Kiara was feeling down. She introduced herself to Kiara and tried to make some small talk.

"So, have you been to India before or is this your first time?" the passenger asked.

"I was born in India, and I have traveled back several times to visit my family," replied Kiara. Normally she would be more interested in socializing, but she was not in a very social mood right now.

"So, you still have family in India?" asked the passenger.

"Yes, but ever since my grandparents passed away, I am not that close to the rest of my relatives there," Kiara replied.

"Are you visiting them this trip?"

"No, I am actually going to see an old friend," said Kiara.

"Oh, do you and your friend have anything special, or fun planned?" the passenger asked.

"Not really. She recently left her husband. He was not a good man. I'm helping her get rid of some old ghosts," said Kiara.

"Oh, wow. I am sorry to hear that. Did he cheat on her?"

"No, he beat her. It started early in their marriage. Initially, he was sweet and loving, but after a few months into their marriage, he started controlling her. He beat and strangled her so badly that he nearly killed her. She forgave him each time because he cried and promised to never to do it again. After years of ignoring it, tolerating it, and forgiving him, she finally began to understand that he was not going to stop and that he is an abusive man by nature." Kiara said in a sad tone.

"Did she tell her family and friends or report it to the police?"

"At first she was too ashamed to tell her family and friends. She was embarrassed and thought the abuse was all her fault. She stayed with him for a long time," Kiara told her.

"Your friend is a very brave woman," said the passenger.

"She thinks she is a coward, a failure. She keeps blaming herself. She thinks she is such a foolish woman for letting this happen to her," Kiara said.

"Foolish? Not at all. It takes a lot of courage to break out of the cycle of abuse and leave that relationship. Your friend is a survivor. A real survivor."

"Really?" Kiara asked, and the passenger nodded her head.

After a two-minute silence, the passenger asked, "So, how long were you married to him?"

"Too long," Kiara said softly as she put her head down on the window. She managed to fall asleep.

After the long flight, she landed at Goa International Airport and took a cab to the city of Mapusa where the retreat was located. The car ride was peaceful, and Kiara took in the beauty of the beaches, ferry boats, and palm trees as they drove. An hour later, she reached the retreat and checked into the Chakra Room. It was the most luxurious room she had ever stayed in, with tropical lush gardens right outside, vibrant natural light, Goan-Portuguese combined with Rajasthani architecture, and a private balcony overlooking the beach.

She rested for a day and then, was ready to join in the retreat activities. Over the next week, Kiara attended yoga classes on the beach, meditation, and mindfulness lectures, received ayurvedic massage treatments, and attended healing hypnotherapy workshops. One of the wellness lectures she attended was entitled "Heal from Trauma and Transform Your Life". It was conducted by a spiritual teacher who was also a holistic leader named Gurvi Sia Das. Gurvi Sia Das grew up in Sri Lanka, but for the last thirty years, she had been teaching this class all throughout India. Her class was geared towards intense people who were hustling in the competitive corporate world or living in chaotic, stressful homes. Through these sessions, she had healed people who had experienced lost or unfulfilled love, sexual or physical abuse, depression or suicidal thoughts, fears, obsessive thoughts, abandonment, and so forth.

Kiara did not know what to expect from this lecture. Before the session began, she took the opportunity to talk to the other participants and heard so many inspirational stories. For example, one gentleman told her about his nephew who was an undocumented immigrant who saved a child dangling from a balcony. Another woman told her about a little boy who raised over a million dollars to help find a cure for his friend's rare disease. Hearing these stories brought tears to Kiara's eyes and filled her heart with empathy. They made her realize that there is so much love and kindness in this world. She needs to let go of her anger and negativity.

As the session began, she walked into the crowded room and sat on the floor mat with the rest of the students while they listened to Gurvi Sia speak. Gurvi Sia was a thin petite woman with a loud but calming tone of voice. Gurvi Sia sat down on the stage, grabbed her microphone, and began the class.

"Good morning, ladies and gentlemen. It is my great honor and privilege to be here with all of you. So, there was a time when my mind was very restless and disturbed. When your emotional state of mind is disturbed, you cannot sleep, you do not eat the way you should, and you do not notice the many pleasures of life. What we forget is that we have the power to control our negative thoughts before those thoughts control us," said Gurvi Sia.

As she continued speaking, she asked volunteers to come up and share stories of their personal adversities. Because the purpose of this session was to heal from a trauma, speaking about it was one way to let go. Out of the one hundred attendees, it appeared no one was ready to share their story. That was when Kiara remembered what Diane taught her: "To let go of painful flashbacks, you need to confront your inner demons by talking about them; that's how those demons will fear you and go away. You need to confront your discomfort." Nervously, Kiara raised her hand, and Gurvi Sia asked her to stand in front of the room next to her and share her story.

"Hello, my name is Kiara, and I am forty-three years old. I have dealt with a lot of rejection, emotional damage, and mental torture my whole life, and I really am kind of lost at this point in my life. As a child, I was very timid and weak and suffered a lot of emotional abuse and racism in school. The bullying and harassment got so bad at school that I even became suicidal at one point, but luckily, God was looking over me."

As Kiara was speaking, she saw that all the participants were focused on her and some were in tears. Kiara continued, "Then at twenty-two years old, I had an arranged marriage. My parents had the most honorable intentions in setting me up. I tried but, I could not accept a man I was not in love with, so I filed for divorce and started a new life.

"Years later, I met another man, and we dated a couple of years. It was a very effortless relationship where he put me on a pedestal and treated me so lovingly, promising me such a happy future. We got married, and a few months into the marriage, he hit me. I forgave him, and then after our second wedding anniversary, we got into a fight, and he ended up beating me so badly that I almost did not live to see my thirty-fifth birthday. That beating went on and off for almost two hours . . . he banged my head against the bed's headboard, pinned me down, and strangled me so badly that my voice turned hoarse and robotic. I was almost killed by him. The only thing I repeatedly said was, 'Please don't kill me, my parents need me. I can't breathe.' After he let me go, he bawled his eyes out and promised to never hit me again. I forgave him.

"Then years later, he beat and strangled me again, and after he cried and apologized, I forgave him. Months later, he hit me again, and I forgave him again. He continuously mistreated me physically, emotionally, psychologically. He treated me like his servant, until one day I packed all my luggage, and left.

As Kiara finished sharing, the room fell silent. Once again you could have heard a pin drop. Then the audience stood and proceeded to overwhelm Kiara with a standing ovation. Gurvi Sia spoke. "I have treated many individuals who had similar stories. It is easy for people to say that if a woman is in an abusive marriage, she should just leave. What they do not understand is that it is not that simple to leave this type of relationship. It is not easy to stand up and share such delicate parts of your life in front of a live audience, and I am sure your story helped someone in this room. You should be proud of yourself because you are a warrior."

As Kiara wiped her tears, she suddenly realized that this moment, this place was exactly the stage she talked so passionately about as her happy place in therapy with Diane. As someone who did not like to talk about her adversities, she was finally recognizing herself as a warrior.

After the session ended, a few of the audience members came up to Kiara as she walked out of the room. "That was such an incredibly powerful story. You are an extremely brave woman," they told her.

"Thank you. I appreciate that," she responded.

They were a group of three American women who had been practicing yoga and spiritual healing for the last twenty years. As they made small talk with Kiara, they mentioned going to a Buddhist temple, which was an hour away from their retreat. "Would you like to join us?

We are going tomorrow morning and will be back by late evening. I am sure visiting this temple will help you in your healing process," they said.

"Sure, I would love to join you. I have never been to a Buddhist temple before, nor do I know anything about Buddhism, but I would love to go and learn something new," she said. There were only a few days left in her trip, and she wanted to see as much as she could.

After a two-hour drive to an isolated area in the mountains, they reached the monastery called the Bodhicitta Temple. The temple was a *stupa* (a mound-like structure) designed to symbolize the five elements: fire, air, earth, water, and wisdom. The main hall was in the center surrounded by a ceremonial bell and drums, and other facilities, including the celestial and the abbot's rooms, on each side. The temple was palatial in appearance and overlooked a beautiful river and stunning mountains. The scene was breathtaking. Being in such a Zen-like ambience, Kiara realized she was not in Kansas anymore!

The temple bell rang at 10 a.m. sharp, as it was time to start the mid-morning meditation and prayer chant ceremony. A line of monks walked together towards the Phra Ubosot (Ordination Hall). The temple abbot, Banko, who administered the day-to-day activities, introduced himself to Kiara and her group and invited them to the chant ceremony, so they all headed towards the Phra Ubosot. They removed their shoes when they walked in, they saw the monks sitting on floor mats in a large circle, and a bowl filled with holy water surrounded by incense, candles, and fruits in the middle of the circle.

Kiara and her friends sat next to the monks on the floor, closed their eyes, and prayed as the chant ceremony began. The whole room chanted together, and Kiara felt so soothed she began to cry. The purity chants brought out the intense feelings of every event that happened in her life, the good, the bad, and the painful ugly. It felt like she was in heaven. After the chanting was over, there was a moment of silence as they began meditation with flute music playing in the background. Kiara's soul felt cleansed as she absorbed the energy of the sacred temple. She got to witness the pure love and spirituality that these monks shared with each other.

After the ceremony was over, the group walked over to the large Buddha statue and bowed down to it. The abbot, Banko, explained, "The Buddha represents the human mind, peace, and profound wisdom. Buddhism is a philosophy that suggests that the awakened wisdom in the Buddha is possible for human beings also." Afterward, the group resumed walking around the temple, but Kiara sat down by herself in front of the Buddha statue. She wanted to be left alone for a moment of silence and solitude. Near the statue, she saw a quote that said, "How people treat you is their karma; how you react to it is yours." That thought-provoking quote triggered her to close her eyes, meditate, and think about her own karma. As someone who did not consider herself particularly religious, and who rarely visited Hindu temples, Kiara was trying to understand and analyze her own relationship with God.

Growing up in a conservative Hindu household, she used to be deeply religious. In fact, right from childhood until early adulthood, Kiara fasted for all religious Hindu holidays and prayed at sunrise and sunset. During the Hindu holiday seasons, she went to the temple daily to offer her devotion and seek blessings. She was so devoted to God because, somewhere in her heart, she thought it would help her become a better human. But now, her views on religion had changed, and she did not feel like devoting herself to God anymore.

Kiara believed God existed and she had received countless blessings: a loving family and great friends, a fulfilling career, financial security, and good health. But outside of these, it felt like her resilience was constantly tested despite proving herself repeatedly.

Now, she was beginning to think that being a good or bad person had more do with karma than it did following strict religious rules. Instead of only seeing the good in the world, she was beginning to see the bad also, which was making her question her blind faith. She kept thinking,

- *Is God as great as people think? Has this supernatural power that none of us have even seen only done good for humanity?*
- *Why do people suffer from cancer and other incurable diseases?*
- *Why is there poverty?*
- *Why are there natural disasters?*

As paradoxical as it sounded, she considered herself to be a God-fearing woman who felt disconnected from God. She just had difficulty devoting herself to a God who inflicted such cruelties on mankind.

Kiara believed that humans carried some positive and negative energies from the karma of their previous lives as well. There were those who, no matter how evil and deceiving, consistently had fortunate circumstances work in their favor. On the contrary, there were those who were charitable and pure-hearted but often fell victim to unfortunate circumstances. The common notion of "what goes around comes around" did not catch up with everyone. Mysteriously, a lot of truly evil people who deserved a taste of their own medicine were off the hook. Could it be karmic energies from their previous lives?

Kiara was in no position to call herself a good or bad person. Although she tried her hardest to be good, she knew she may have hurt people in the past who might disagree. At the same time, being good or bad was subjective, so that judgement should be best left up to God.

She also thought about Angad and how he was a deeply religious Hindu who fasted, prayed, visited the temple frequently, and did not eat beef (cows are sacred to Hindus). Does that mean he is a pure person? A man who beat and almost killed a woman should not be considered good.

Kiara believed that being religious did not automatically grant people entrance to heaven nor that being an atheist condemned them to hell. She just kept thinking about how much an abusive marriage and other adversities taught her about her own personal karma.

To confess, she had made her share of mistakes and may have hurt people in the past. At the same time, she had also helped so many others, gave charitable donations, and did countless good deeds as an aunt, sister, daughter, friend, and human. *But why does reaping the fruits of good karma always take longer to catch up to her than the mistakes of bad karma?* Tears flowed down her face as she frustratingly thought about her good and bad karma.

Kiara was starting to understand that it took years of fighting off her own inner demons and insecurities to begin to recognize her own personal karma. And at this point, the deep complexities of karma and why things happened the way they did remained a mystery.

Maybe someday in a perfect world when things such as cancer and other incurable diseases, poverty, and natural disasters miraculously disappeared, she would feel more comfortable bowing down to God. Being present in such a sacred land such as the Bodhicitta, she felt more detached from religion and more attached to her spiritual well-being.

After thirty minutes of meditation, Kiara took a walk outside on the hillside when it suddenly began raining. She always loved rainy weather, but this experience was like nothing before. After she walked through the hazy puddles towards the top of the hill, she stopped there-- soaking in the atmosphere, feeling like she was on top of the world! Standing on the hill, she fully embraced the rain, fog, and wind and felt a miraculous sense of power within herself as if, braving the storms of her own life. It felt like the rain was washing away the damages of a lifetime, and she was making peace with and falling in love with herself. During this moment, Kiara remembered a time when she told Diane that she was fearful of going through the process of divorce from Angad because she had gotten used to having a significant other in her life and that starting a new life as a single woman was terribly scary.

Then Diane told her a story. "You know, when I go over to watch my granddaughter when her parents are out of town for the weekend, she feels sad and lonely without them. However, she finds ways to spend her time playing, eating, studying, and just keeping herself busy. Then after the weekend is over and her parents are back home again, she realizes that she did a great job of taking care of herself all on her own without their help. Being alone feels intimidating to you right now, but when you think about it, you have been alone for a good portion of your life and have already learned how to protect yourself. You are much stronger and braver than you think."

Here in this holy place, Kiara realized that, --by being isolated and rejected by others, she has, indeed, been on her own her whole life. During her younger days, she was alone and very lonely. Today as an adult, she is choosing to be alone without a husband and is fully embracing her solitude. Maybe this was a big part of her self-realization that she finally recognized during this trip.

It was almost time for Kiara and her group to head back to their retreat. The Goa trip was coming to an end. The days she spent praying, traveling, learning, meditating, and interacting with others felt so rejuvenating that she was finally starting to let go of painful memories. Before this trip, Kiara felt like a woman defeated by life. But by the end of the trip, she felt like a victorious woman who had triumphantly emerged a powerful survivor.

# CHAPTER TEN

# Turning Over a New Leaf

"You should never view your challenges as a
disadvantage. Instead, it's important for you to understand
that your experience facing and overcoming adversity
is actually one of your biggest advantages"

**–Michelle Obama**

Kiara returned from her trip at the end of June 2018. The trip to India was such a life-changing experience that Kiara felt less fearful about confronting her marital issues. The issues and problems that had blurred her inner vision for so long were now starting to clear. When she first began dating Angad, he never once gave her the slightest indication that he was a controlling, abusive, and narcissistic man. In fact, hiding these negative traits is something narcissistic and abusive people are great at doing. During their courtship, he did not show any red flags. Now, Kiara is realizing that having no red flag could be a red flag.

What happened to all those nice things he told her such as, "I feel like a fish out of water when we don't talk," or "I promise to give you a happy and bright future," or "If anyone has something rude to say to you, they will have to get past me first."? When she remembers his exact words, her blood boils. This man used her and mentally and physically abused her. Angad treated her as if she were worthless and as though he had no use for her. But he did not want her to leave him because that meant losing power over her.

Diane once told her, "I am going to say something harsh, but it is important. Your husband lied to you. He lied about who he really was, what his real motives were, and how he was going to treat you. He put on a nice guy act for as long as he could, but it was a classic case of bait and switch. Right after you two were married, --he had finally gotten you and that is when he showed you the truth about him. Narcissists purposely target people they view as vulnerable, and that is what he did to you."

Today Kiara understands this insight because she feels Angad truly did lie, covered up his motives, and deceived her all along.

### On her spiritual journey,
### Kiara learned so much about herself. She learned:

- Her personality is not a good fit for a permanent relationship like a marriage.
- She is a lot stronger as a single woman than a married one.
- She will never again tolerate, ignore, or forgive a man who disrespects her and her family.
- If a man mistreats or misbehaves with her, she will no longer hide or cover up for him.
- Her views on marriage have dramatically changed. Obviously, she knows many marriages that are strong and long-lasting, so not all of them are difficult. Just because she had a tough experience does not mean she will discourage others from marrying. As much as she tried to avoid a divorce, Kiara now feels that marriage just may not be her thing anymore.

As Kiara looked back on all she had been through, she asked herself:

- *Why was I always to blame when something went wrong? Marriage is supposed to be a two-way street.*
- *Why was cooking and cleaning only my responsibility?*
- *Was I really a bad wife just because I was a bad cook?*
- *Why did I wake up from my naps in the middle of a splitting migraine just to prepare food for him?*
- *Why did I have to beg and plead to him for something as basic as visiting my family?*
- *Why was I always the one to make compromises and sacrifices?*
- *Why were all my wishes and desires consistently rejected by him?*

The only time Kiara was happy in her marriage was when her relationship was long-distance. During those phases, many people (especially women) could not believe she lived apart from her husband. They had a hard time understanding how she lived and worked in a different state from her husband. Their relationship was good when they lived apart, so sometimes she thinks, she should not have rocked the boat by moving in with him. Despite modifying her life several times to accommodate Angad's career, ambitions, and dreams, he never treated her with any dignity. The misogynist in him believed it was the wife's duty to follow wherever her husband went and prioritize him over everything else.

Kiara's marriage to Angad also influenced her understanding of the patriarchy. Google defines patriarchy as: *a system of society or government in which men hold the power and women are largely excluded from it.* However, while Kiara did not let Angad taint her image of all men, she had a problem with men being given institutional power and control of the world. Kiara does not believe in patriarchy, matriarchy, or any system or relationship where one gender holds the power. She believes men and women should have equal power.

Society teaches us to believe that marriage and kids are part of the cycle of life, and without these two things, women are incomplete. It wants us to think that our self-worth, purpose, and happiness are only valid once we sign a marriage contract and have children. These deceiving theories merely disguise the expectations that women should be responsible for the happiness of their homes. Why can't the responsibility of making or breaking a home be shared by both the husband and wife?

These disparities fall back significantly on one thing: how boys and girls are raised. If children observe their fathers, grandfathers, and uncles go to work, come home, eat dinner, watch TV, and go to sleep, they will grow up to think this is what men are supposed to do. And if children see their mothers, grandmothers, and aunts cook, clean, go to work, and rush back from work to cook and clean again, they will grow up to think this is what women are supposed to do. Furthermore, if they see violence in the household during their childhood, they grow up believing this behavior is normal and blame the victim. Growing up in a traditional and male-dominated family in India, these were the values instilled in Angad's mind.

What Kiara is learning is that patriarchy is a big part of the South Asian culture. Even most Hindu traditions appear to be rooted in inequality. She recalled watching an interview with Kamala Bhasin, a feminist Indian author who questioned the Raksha Bandhan tradition where a sister ties rakhi (thread) on her brother's wrist. "Why don't brothers tie a rakhi on their sisters for Raksha Bandhan?"

During this holiday, sisters tie a thread called rakhi on their brother's wrist as a symbol of his protection of her, and she prays for his wellness in return.

But why, Kiara wonders, is it expected only for sisters to tie a rakhi on their brothers? Brothers and sisters both vow to shield each other, so why should only the brother be put on a pedestal and be given this honor? There are so many stories narrating how the tradition of Raksha Bandhan started. No matter which version you choose to follow, the bottom line is that, before a man goes out to fight a battle, his sister (or another woman in the family) would tie a thread on his wrist and pray for his victory. It is understandable why this concept began centuries ago since women were not allowed to fight in wars back then. But modern society allows both men and women to fight in wars. If a sister can now also fight for her brother, doesn't she deserve the same respect and honor as him?

What is funny is when an older sister ties a rakhi on their younger brother without expecting the same in return . . . is that the older sister most likely was the one who helped her parents take care of her younger brother ever since he was a baby. She is the one who nurtured him like a second mother and guarded him from bullies on the playground. Yet only he has the honor of having a rakhi tied on him and not her. Kiara and her family celebrated this holiday her entire life. But today, she is starting to question its inequality.

Kiara reflects on a few other Hindu rituals that prioritize men over women: Karva Chauth, Bhai Dooj, Teej, and Jamai Sashti, just to name a few. Karva Chauth is where a wife fasts and prays for her husband's long life; Bhai Dooj is where sisters do the same for their brothers. There is also Teej, which again is observed for the wellness of one's husband or a loving future husband. Jamai Sashti is celebrated, where the women in the house celebrate the son-in-law.

If marriage is all about partnership and equality, then why can't these rituals be equalized? There is one sign of progression- during Karva Chauth it is now common for husbands to fast for their wives.

However, Kiara thinks, adopting a few traditions that celebrate just women would be real progress. The thing is, even if Kiara expresses her support for celebrating a feminist Raksha Bandhan, she understands that in the beginning it will probably feel strange for a sister to have a rakhi tied on her, that is only because society is not used to this ritual. Kiara wishes Indian society would recognize the double standard in these holidays and traditions that encourage patriarchy. Change has to begin somewhere.

Once her therapist, Diane, told her that her experiences had created an activist in her, which Kiara never understood until it happened to her. Today on her spiritual journey, she understands it and wants to implement change starting in her own family.

Another thing Kiara previously struggled to understand is how Angad or any human develops abusive tendencies. Is it just anger management issues or something more? During one of the therapy sessions, Diane explained that Angad's abusive tendencies had to do with his inner demons and how he was raised.

"Nothing you did caused the abuse. This is exclusively a problem within the abuser. Even if your husband moves on and marries another woman, he will still have those same abusive tendencies because the problem is not the woman he is with, but within himself," explained Diane.

Kiara decides to forgive herself for taking the blame all those years. She now sees that violence against women is not just a woman's issue, but a man's issue as well. Men, she believes, should be equally responsible for creating a safe and healthy home. She realized that many of the behaviors she tolerated reflected what she had learned from a patriarchal culture and society. She just accepted them because of her shy and nonconfrontational nature. But Kiara wanted to break this patriarchal chain and set a better example for other women, especially for the next generation of women in her family.

Kiara decides to live her life in an unconventional manner: to question, and possibly disrupt the status quo. She realizes that some may criticize her choices at times, still she is committed to creating the change.

# CHAPTER ELEVEN

# Independence Day

"Don't ever stop. Keep going.
If you want a taste of freedom, keep going."

**—Harriet Tubman**

ooking back, it is amazing how many ups and downs Kiara has gone through. Today, she lives with her family in the suburbs of Sacramento, has a great career, and socializes with friends whenever she wants. The freedom and independence that she lost for a while, she finally got back again. As a child, Kiara never thought she would be in an abusive marriage. At the same time, this is not her identity, nor does it define her as a person. The marital struggles she went through were only segments of her life, not her entire life.

She had spent the last several weeks mentally processing the good, the bad, and the ugly side of marriage, but now it was time to finally make the life-altering decision of officially staying or leaving this marriage. On one hand, if she stayed, she could relocate back to Texas and resume cycling through the power and control used against her. Most likely, nothing would change in terms of Angad's treatment of her. On the other hand, she could choose to file for divorce and start a new life where she did not have to answer to anyone. She thought to herself, *If I had a daughter who was in my shoes, what would I advise her to do? What advice would I give to any woman in my shoes?*

She did not want to be a hypocrite by advocating for women's rights while staying with an abusive man. As a survivor, she wanted to help pave the way for other women like her. There must be so many women (and even men) who had gone through, were currently going through, or knew others who had experienced exactly what she had. Sadly, because of society's expectations, many of these individuals were suffering silently behind closed doors, just as she had.

Kiara takes a moment to contemplate an email she recently received from Angad. It was a sweet and loving email apologizing and saying that he missed her. She really appreciated the nice note and was open to seeing him. It had been over a month, so they both had time and space apart. Angad offered to purchase a plane ticket for her return to Austin. Kiara decided to take this opportunity to see him and booked her trip for the 4th of July weekend.

After landing in Austin, she took an Uber to Angad's house. When Kiara showed up at his door, she found that Angad was ecstatic to see her.

"It is really nice to see you, Kiara! How are you?" he asked.

"I am doing well. How are you?" she asked.

"Hey, please come inside. Let us talk," he said as she walked in and sat down on the sofa. She saw he had two cups of coffee and her favorite pastries on the coffee table. She was pleasantly surprised by how formal and cordial he was behaving. "So how has your summer been so far?" Angad asked.

"Very nice, actually. I just got back from India," she responded.

"Oh, that's nice. Where did you go? Did you go with your parents?" he asked.

"No, I went alone and just toured Goa." she replied.

"Well, Goa is a crazy beach party town, so I am sure you must have some met someone nice there," Angad said jokingly.

"Yes, actually I did meet someone nice there. —I met myself," replied Kiara with a gentle smile.

After spending some time talking about her trip and catching up, Angad said, "Kiara, I really miss you. I am so sorry for the fight we had last time. I do not even remember what the fight was about. I just want you to move back with me and we will start a new life all over again," he told her.

"If I moved back here, would you come visit me or my family in Sacramento?" she asked.

Angad hesitated before answering. "I have already explained to you many times that I will never visit there again."

Angad spent the next ten minutes trying to persuade her to move back with him again. He told her that as a woman, she was not strong enough to live the rest of her life without him. She needed him as her protector.

"Truthfully, I doubt that you ever loved me," she said in reply.

"That is not true. I have always treated you with love and respect," he countered her opinion.

"I do not love you. And I do not think you ever loved me because love should not hurt psychologically, financially, physically, or any other way," she replied.

"That is not true. I loved and respected you. You just never listened to me. You always provoked my anger and then acted like the victim. If you never caused my anger, I would not react that way," he told her.

By now, Kiara had lost interest in responding. She simply reached into her bag, pulled out a box and handed it to him. When Angad opened this box, he saw it contained their wedding photos and videos, jewelry, her mangalsutra (nuptial necklace), small wedding gifts, and other items she saved all these years. He looked confused.

Kiara looked at him without smiling. "Angad. I just met with a lawyer and am officially filing for divorce. I want to personally return these items to you. It's over." With that, she stood up and walked over to the door.

"I wish you a happy, healthy, and successful life. Goodbye," Kiara opened the door, walked out of his house for the last time and never looked back.

The reason she went to see Angad was to bring things to a closure, make this decision in person, and prove that she finally had her power and control back. She will always fondly remember July 4th as her personal Independence Day.

• •

After filing for divorce and leaving old ghosts behind, Kiara was finally ready for a fresh new start in life. She planned to continue seeing her therapist, Diane, who was now her life coach. Although she had come a long way from being the timid little girl, the insecure young woman, the powerless wife, and now a survivor of adversities, she still had a long way to go in this spiritual journey of self-discovery, self-empowerment, and bravery.

Kiara has learned to let go of her anger and resentment. She has found a place in her heart to forgive anyone who has hurt her in the past. Although forgiving Angad may take some more time. Forgiveness is less about the other person and more about finding peace within yourself. Just as she was speaking to her younger self, Kiara now understands that there is a lot of love, compassion, and empathy in the world despite her tough experiences. There are good people in the world. She has also forgiven herself for any mistakes she has made. Kiara wants the world to know the authentic woman she is. Yes, she may still wear her heart on her sleeve, but it truly is a heart of gold.

Kiara went to see Diane a few days after meeting Angad, and Diane was so happy not only to see how much progress Kiara had made, but to learn that Kiara had mustered the strength to finally file for divorce. Diane said, "You are on the brink of being a very happy woman." When Kiara heard those words, she instantly cried. But this time they were tears of joy.

Moving forward, she wants to do everything that she was held back from for all these years. She wants to be a world traveler and experience different cultures, food, people, and scenery. She may even visit another Buddhist temple as she continues this path of soul searching. Another important goal of Kiara's is to be involved in nonprofits that specialize in treating abuse victims and survivors so that she can help others recover from trauma the way she did. She also hopes to give a TED Talk someday so that she can share her story of adversity and bravery to help others. Although she feels she will never want to get married again, she is open to explore romantic experiences. She may even write a book about those escapades. — Another step on her brave journey through life!

# Sample References and Resources

*note to my readers:*

*The stories shared in this book are not intended to fully describe specific medical treatments nor are they meant as recommendations. Please refer to appropriate medical professionals for information and treatment.*

As Kiara continued her therapy sessions, it became necessary for her to look back at her relationship with Angad and the behaviors she experienced. To help her process what she was learning, she began researching domestic violence as well. Wikipedia defines domestic violence as: "violence or other abuse in a domestic setting, such as in marriage or cohabitation. It is often used as a synonym for intimate partner violence."

As Kiara continued her therapy sessions, it became necessary for her to look back at her relationship with Angad and the behaviors she experienced. To help her process what she was learning, she began researching domestic violence as well. Wikipedia defines domestic violence as: "violence or other abuse in a domestic setting, such as in marriage or cohabitation. It is often used as a synonym for intimate partner violence."

The first thing she learned was the **Cycle of Abuse**. (See diagram by Dr. Lenore E. Walker on reference page).

## Phase 1—Tension Building

The abuser gradually becomes irritable and gets angry even over the most miniscule things. The victim walks on eggshells around the abuser in fear that the abuser will explode at any minute.

## Phase 2—Explosion Happens

The abuser reaches the maximum limit of anger and irritability and as a result, physical or sexual violence takes place. In situations where the abuse does not turn physical or sexual, the perpetrator will turn aggressive towards the victim emotionally, mentally, or verbally.

## Phase 3—Reconciliation Takes Place

During this phase, the abuser starts feeling guilty and regretful. In most cases, the victim leaves or plans to leave the relationship, but the abuser apologizes profusely, promising, "It'll never happen again." During this cycle, the victim also feels like he or she has the power in the relationship because their abuser now puts them on a pedestal.

## Phase 4—Everything is Calm

This is the honeymoon phase when the abuser becomes overly loving and generous towards their significant other. The abuser showers the victim with gifts and apologies. The victim believes the abuser will never mistreat them again, so they decide to stay in the relationship. Little does the victim realize that it is just a matter of time until the abuser goes back to the first phase of the cycle.

Another topic Kiara learned about was the **Battered Woman Syndrome**. (See list/website by Dr. Lenore E. Walker on Reference page) The more Kiara read about the syndrome, the more she recognized it in her own life. For instance, she kept reexperiencing the abusive events in her mind, tried numbing her emotions, experienced hyperarousal of mind and body, disrupted relationships with friends and family and had issues with health and body image.

In addition:

1. **Guilt:** Each time Angad put his hands on her, she genuinely thought she provoked him to behave that way. Because he immediately cried and apologized, her heart melted. She thought, *I am such a bad wife. My husband is such a kind-hearted soul who never hurts anyone, and I keep bringing out the worst in him. I provoke him to do this to me. It is all my fault.* Because she felt so guilty, she blamed herself for the abuse.

2. **Denial:** Deep down, she knew Angad could be scary and violent, but for a long time, she refused to consider him abusive. Google defines abusive as: "engaging in or characterized by habitual violence and cruelty." Kiara realized that Diane had helped her recognize that she had been in denial during her entire marriage to Angad. Even during those phases when she had left him, she could not admit to herself that he was abusive. Kiara thought that their incidents were bad fights and something that all married couples experience.

3. **Enlightenment:** October 2017 was a turning point for Kiara because this was when the #MeToo movement exploded. Although this movement was, primarily, based around sexual abuse and assault, the stories about women silently suffering and protecting their abusers resonated with her. The more she heard stories and interviews in the media about victims and survivors, the more she started to make comparisons

with her own life. During this time, she was also watching the HBO series *Big Little Lies*.

In the series, one of the main characters is a female victim of intimate partner violence and viewers witness her journey as she moves from denial to realization. Watching those difficult scenes about the abused wife triggered Kiara as she found similarities in her own situation which made her question herself: *Am I being controlled? Is the violence I am experiencing not normal? Am I not at fault?*

In December 2017, when Kiara had her annual gynecological appointment and she completed the healthcare questionnaire, she decided for the first time in a long time to answer the questions about abuse honestly. After reviewing that form, her doctor immediately said, "Kiara, I had no idea these things happened to you. Your husband is not a good person. I see that you have been experiencing itching, hair loss, and migraines. And your blood pressure is extremely high. I suspect the emotional and physical stress is the cause of most, if not all, of your symptoms. I can run some tests and will prescribe some medications to help you with these symptoms. Some of these medicines you may need to take for the rest of your life because the symptoms are so severe. Do you realize the mental and emotional stress you are dealing with in your marriage is affecting your physical health?" Kiara quietly listened and did not have much to say. She felt embarrassed but realized her doctor was only giving her tough love.

"Angad, my husband, is actually moving to Texas next month," Kiara said.

"I hope you are not moving with him. Are you?" asked her doctor.

"No, I do not want to move with him again. I accepted a job offer from a company in my hometown of Sacramento. I am moving back with my family."

"Good. Any man who raises his hand to a woman, especially the woman he claims to love, is not a good person. Your husband is not a good person. Do you have a secret code?"

"What do you mean?" Kiara asked in confusion.

"A secret code is something victims use as an escape plan. It could be signal to others. An example is a phone call to the police on the pretext of ordering pizza delivery, for example. Anything along those lines you can think of. You need to leave him, and I suggest you talk to a specialist. We will provide you with some information" her doctor firmly stated.

This was an enlightening moment for Kiara. She held herself together in the office, but when she got inside her car, she sobbed. She thought, *Why am I feeling so embarrassed talking to my doctor about my marital issues? His intentions were good; maybe he is right about getting out of this marriage.*

4. **Responsibility:** This was another hard step to manage. The abused feels a responsibility to hold the family together, responsibility to be accountable for his or her behavior that may have added to the problem. Often, the victim forgets that they must also take responsibility for their own happiness and safety.

In Kiara's research of this topic, she also learned about something called **The Power and Control Factors.** (See chart/list by Dr. Lenore E. Walker on Reference page). This list is divided into various sections describing how an abuser gains and maintains power and control over their intimate partner.

Of the sections on this list, the ones that resonated with her the most were isolation, jealousy, and emotional/psychological abuse.

1. **Isolation:** This was the biggest one. Abuse thrives in isolation. Isolating Kiara from her loved ones was Angad's main way of controlling her. Kiara's phone calls to her family, homesickness,

and her desire to return to California always sparked anger in Angad. At one point he even tried convincing her to move to Canada by saying, "The job market in Canada is really strong. You can easily find marketing jobs in Toronto. We can live very comfortably there." He wanted her to only depend on him, which was easier when she was geographically distant from her family.

2. **Jealousy:** One time when Kiara and Angad went to the movie theater, another man came and sat next to her. After the movie was over, Angad spent the entire night screaming and cursing about how she let another man sit next to her. He accused her of moving closer to the other man and touching him.

"If you would rather be with another man, then you need to divorce me now," he told her in anger.

"I did not touch him. I do not want to divorce you. I did not do anything wrong. I am so sorry I let another man sit next to me. Please do not divorce me. I am so sorry," she begged and pleaded for his forgiveness.

His jealousy was even worse when it came to her family. He was so jealous of the strong relationship Kiara had with her entire family that he tried instigating things against all of them. He would say things such as, "Your family members only talk to you because your parents are alive. Once they pass away, the other family members will all kick you out of the house. They have their own lives, so you are a burden to them. That is why I keep saying that you need to only depend on me because I will always be around."

Obviously, Kiara did not believe him, but she was appalled at how badly he continuously spoke about her family. He always had a good deal of animosity toward her parents, and he accused them of influencing her to live away from him. "What kind of parents let their married daughter live in their house away from her husband?!" he would yell.

Angad even hated how Kiara's extended family constantly hosted parties. Growing up, his family did not host or attend parties, so he was uncomfortable in that type of social atmosphere. Anytime she attended a family party, his blood boiled. He expected her to boycott these parties just the way he did.

3.  **Psychological Abuse (mind control, verbal, and mental put down):**

     Another aspect of domestic violence, Kiara now understands, is that she was also a victim of emotional and psychological abuse. It is a common misconception that domestic violence is only physical abuse. Before Angad physically abused her, he had already crossed the boundaries of abusing her emotionally and mentally. It angered Kiara to think back on how she overlooked the mental and emotional attacks she suffered.

     For example:

a.  **Her weight:** Today, when she thinks about when they first met, she wonders, *Was he ever even physically attracted to me?* Throughout their relationship, Angad relentlessly insulted Kiara's weight. In college, she used to weigh almost one hundred sixty pounds. It took a lot of blood, sweat, and tears to knock off thirty pounds. During the time she dated Angad, she weighed a healthy one hundred twenty-five pounds and was a size four. Just six months into their relationship, he told her to lose weight before meeting his family. As he laid on the sofa with one arm on his forehead, he repeatedly expressed disappointment in her weight.

     "Can you please go on a diet and start exercising? You need to lose weight before meeting my parents. I am so worried that when my family meets you, they will think you are not skinny enough for me," he said.

She felt very hurt and insulted by his words and could not believe he said these things. After some silence, she was in tears.

"Please don't say this to me. I do not think I am fat at all. I have lost a lot of weight the last few years. That is a mean and cruel thing to say to me," she responded emotionally.

Angad saw her tears but did not care. He was so worried that he was about to get married to a woman who was not skinny enough for him. He told her they needed to postpone their trip to meet his family so that she had more time to lose weight. When Kiara told this story to her therapist, Diane said, "He only wanted you to lose weight so that it could make his image look good. This is exactly what narcissists do." Today when Kiara looks back at this situation, it makes her angry because now she understands that this was just another example of him trying to control her.

Even throughout their marriage, she did her best to eat healthy (especially around him) and joined the gym. Angad would still say things like, "The gym will not make a difference because you do not know how to work out." Anytime she lost weight, she would excitedly tell him, but he showed no reaction as if it was not a big deal. Being married to him made her feel like her appearance was never good enough, and as a result, her self-esteem plummeted drastically.

b.  **Her career:** When Angad moved to New Hampshire and later Texas, he repeatedly threatened to divorce Kiara if she did not quit her job in California to relocate with him. During the initial days of his competitive legal field, he was struggling to get his foot in the door as a corporate attorney. It was Kiara that had always helped to financially support them, yet Angad still expected her to take a significant pay cut and relocate with him wherever he moved. In his view, her career had no value. Even after she had accepted the position with her current employer in 2018, he had said, "Quit your new job and look for jobs in Austin."

"But looking for a new job is time-consuming. You want me to quit my job and stay unemployed in your house until I find a new job?" she rhetorically asked.

"Yes," said Angad.

"I can't do that. I have bills to pay," said Kiara.

"I will pay your bills," Angad replied.

Fortunately, Kiara did not listen to him this time and did not quit her job. Now she understands that if he had taken care of her bills, that would mean he would have had even more power and control over her. Despite letting his other faults slide, Kiara was glad she relentlessly pushed back to maintain her financial independence.

c.  **Patriarchal views:** Growing up in a traditional, male-dominated household in India, Angad was conditioned to think that cooking and cleaning was solely the wife's job. His overall behavior and treatment of Kiara confirmed his chauvinistic mentality.

During the New Hampshire days, Kiara suffered from migraines almost daily. Whenever she took naps, Angad would storm into the room, pull the covers off, and start screaming at her because she had not prepared food for him.

"I am not someone like you who is satisfied with only one meal a day! I need to have breakfast, lunch, and dinner.

Instead of preparing food for me, you are in here sleeping, and I am out there starving!" he would yell. Even when her head pounded with the worst migraines, she would get up just to prepare food for him. When her cooking did not turn out good, he would say, "You are just useless!"

Also, during their time in New Hampshire, Angad worked from home while Kiara's commute was an hour and a half each way. Coming home after a long commute, she was expected to cook dinner even though he had the time to do it working at home all day. On top of that, she was not allowed to prepare ready-made packaged food because it was too unhealthy for him. So, she continued cooking from scratch daily just to keep the peace in the house and avoid being screamed and cursed at. God forbid if Kiara refused to cook; Angad would huff and puff, scold her and report that he was a good husband because he did "her job."

Not only did Angad expect her to do the domestic chores, but he also wanted to control her finances. He was working on paying off his law school student loans and expected her to help him. Kiara had taken on her share of responsibilities for her family ever since she was seventeen years old. She could not just drop all those duties and suddenly add his student loans to her plate. This was a big source of Angad's anger and resulted in him constantly screaming, fighting, and cursing at her about it. This was another way he tried to isolate and detach her from her family so she could focus only on him. Because she refused to help him pay off his student loans, he turned even more bitter towards her and resentful of her family. He had no empathy towards her whatsoever. This was another example of his narcissism, where he thought everything should revolve around him only.

d.  **Denying and blaming:** The first time Kiara heard about narcissism was during her therapy sessions with Diane. Diane described a narcissist as someone who has a delusional sense of self-worth and lacks empathy. Today, Kiara recognizes how precisely that definition applies to Angad's behavior. Throughout the entire marriage, he never once admitted to making a mistake. According to Angad, anything that went wrong was Kiara's fault. Kiara heard so much criticism from him day and night that she started believing that everything, including the violence, was her fault. This behavior is described as gaslighting. According to Psychology Today, gaslighting is "a tactic in which a person or entity, in order to gain more power, makes a victim question their reality."

Kiara was his punching bag and scapegoat for all his mistakes and problems. Anytime he had a bad day at work, heard racist comments by his managing director, or was frustrated by being discriminated against at work, he took all his anger out on her. Anytime he was stressed about his student loans, he blamed Kiara. All the times he beat and choked her, he said she provoked him to lose his temper. Angad saw himself as a gentle man but, blamed Kiara for bringing out the worst in him whenever he got violent.

Anytime she was mad at him for insulting or hurting her feelings, he accused her of being mad at him only because she was missing her family and needed an excuse to go visit them. As a typical narcissist, he just did not have any empathy for her whatsoever. During the initial days of their marriage, Angad found out that one of his good friends completed an accelerated law degree in Europe. He called up Kiara in the middle of work and yelled at her, saying it was her fault that he did not know about this accelerated program. If he did, then he would have graduated a lot sooner. Kiara had no knowledge of this program, either, but it was easier for him blame her than to take responsibility himself.

At one time, Angad had received a job offer from a law firm in New York City. He declined the offer as it was not lucrative enough considering the cost of living in New York. Kiara agreed and consoled him telling him that she did not think it was a good fit, financially.

However, Angad misunderstood her and screamed.

"You didn't want me to accept this job is because you don't want to live far away from your family!" Although he was insulted by the firm's low-ball offer, it was easier to blame Kiara than himself for not accepting the position.

When Kiara suggested couples therapy, he said, "Oh please, there is nothing wrong with me at all. I have not done anything wrong in this relationship. I do not need therapy. You are the one who needs to see ten therapists and they still would not be able to fix you. You would be a big challenge for them," he said mockingly. Being the narcissist that he was, in his eyes he could never do anything wrong, and he was never to blame.

As Kiara completed this in-depth therapy, she became more certain that her decision to leave Angad was the correct one, and she determined never to allow another person to control her life and happiness.

• •

Kiara has now succeeded in becoming responsible for her own happiness and involves herself in activities and causes that help other women become educated in all types of abuse and in the therapy and treatment to help them survive and thrive in their own brave journeys.

# *References*

## Chart developed by Dr. Lenore E. Walker (Psychologist)

https://www.drlenoreewalker.com/

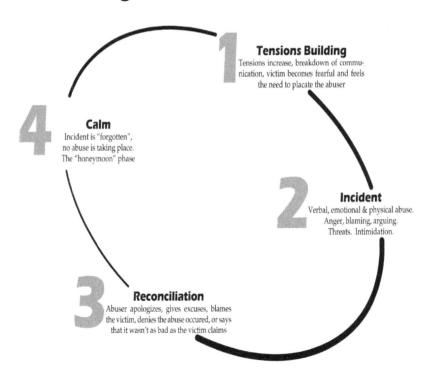

# Cycle of Abuse

**1 Tensions Building**
Tensions increase, breakdown of communication, victim becomes fearful and feels the need to placate the abuser

**4 Calm**
Incident is "forgotten", no abuse is taking place. The "honeymoon" phase

**2 Incident**
Verbal, emotional & physical abuse. Anger, blaming, arguing. Threats. Intimidation.

**3 Reconciliation**
Abuser apologizes, gives excuses, blames the victim, denies the abuse occured, or says that it wasn't as bad as the victim claims

## Lists/Charts developed by Dr. Lenore E. Walker (Psychologist)

https://www.drlenoreewalker.com/

### Battered Woman Syndrome

1. Reexperiencing abusive events in the mind
2. Avoidance Behaviors & Numbing of Emotions
3. Hyperarousal of mind and body
4. Disrupted interpersonal relationships
5. Distorted body image and Physical Health Issues

### Power & Control Factors

1. Isolation
2. Jealousy
3. Intrusive behavior
4. Over possessiveness
5. Psychological/Emotional Abuse
   - Mind control
   - Verbal abuse
   - Mental put downs
   - Debilitating behavior
   - Harassment

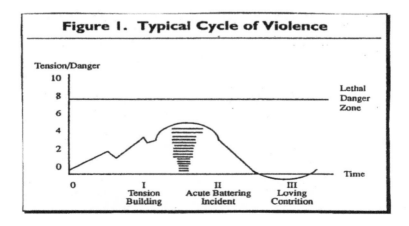

# *Acknowledgments*

N ever in my dreams did I imagine I would actually be a published author someday! Writing a book is not as easy as it looks but is an extremely rewarding experience once you cross the finish line. The biggest lesson I have learned on this journey is that it takes a village to create a published author. There are so many significant people I want to thank for creating the author that I am today.

## SECTION 1:

My father, Nirvya Nand Singh, and mother, Nirmala Singh

I would like to start off by writing a big thank-you note to the following individuals: my father (Nirvya Nand Singh), mother (Nirmala Singh), aunt (Pratima Singh), and uncle (Adyanand Singh).

These individuals made the long and emotional trek from India to the United States to provide a better future for their children. They left behind their parents, family members, and childhood friends, and made so many sacrifices for their children always putting our needs before their own. When they first immigrated to the United States, they all faced the common challenges most immigrants do when moving to a new country. But despite those challenges, they continued working tirelessly and resiliently for their kids, and never once complained even during days when they missed their Motherland.

I still remember my parents' struggles during my childhood. Even during those tough days, my sister and I never lacked for anything. They gave us the same joys, happiness, and comfort as other kids. If I keep thinking about those days and all they gave up for us, I will cry buckets. My mother and father taught me how to walk my first steps, and today I nurture and pamper them. One of the reasons I do not want children of my own is because I have happily taken on the role of being a parent to my aging mother and father. Growing up, I used to be petrified of my dad! But today I realized he is just a delicate teddy bear on the inside. My mother is one of the most kindhearted women I know. Even within our extended family, there is not a single child she has not taken care of. Many people say God comes first in their lives, but for me, my parents are above God. I am so proud to be their daughter.

I also want to express sincere gratitude to my aunt and uncle because my family and I would not be anywhere in our lives if it was not for them. They sponsored me and my family, brought us to the

My aunt, Pratima Singh, and uncle, Adyanand Singh

United States in 1985, and helped us significantly at every step in getting settled here as new immigrants. My aunt and uncle have always treated me and my sister like their daughters, not their nieces. I have always looked up to and respected them as my second set of parents. I especially admire my aunt's emotional strength and my uncle's business acumen and sense of humor! It makes me so emotional when I think about their compassion and how much they have done for me and my family. I love them both dearly from the bottom of my heart and feel very blessed to be their niece.

My mother, father, aunt, and uncle have taught me the power of courage, resilience, selflessness, and unconditional love. It is because of their prayers and sacrifices that I am privileged enough to pursue my dream of being an author. I am forever indebted to all of them for their love and guidance in preparing me to be the woman that I am today. Thank you!

## SECTION 2:

My brother-in-law, Kingsley Kodan, and sister, Minoo Singh Kodan

I want to acknowledge my brother-in-law (Kingsley Kodan) and sister (Minoo Singh Kodan). My brother-in-law has always guided me like an older brother and father figure. I especially want to thank him for helping me refinance all three of my houses! This was an overly complex and time-consuming process that benefited me financially at the end. My brother-in-law gives the best advice on career, finance, real estate, and life, in general. He is a self-made man who has always understood family responsibilities right from a young age and for that, I will always admire and respect him. He is very protective of me and my parents, and we are incredibly lucky to have him as a part of our family.

A very heartfelt thank you to my big sister. Being eight years older than me, she always pampered, protected, and defended me like a lioness mother. Thanks to all the practice she had raising me, she turned out be such a perfect mother to her own two children. Nobody understands my vulnerabilities, weaknesses, and challenges like she does. I am the luckiest sister in the world for having such a strong, honest, and protective and big sister. No matter how much I try, I can never be as nonjudgmental, wise, and compassionate as she is.

I consider anything my sister tells me the ultimate gospel truth. She is the one wiping away my tears, listening to my million problems, believing in me whenever I doubted myself, and always reminding me of my self-worth. My only complaint about her is that one time when I was in fourth grade, she forgot to pick me up from the bus stop, and a Golden Retriever jumped on me. I went home crying to her. Even today, I am still scared of dogs because of that incident! I know I am not an easy person to be around, so I want to thank her for not disowning me! No matter how annoying of a younger sister I can be, she has no choice but to continue loving me.

## SECTION 3:

The best gift my brother-in-law and sister gave me is my niece (Asha Elina Kodan) and nephew (Anish Ethan Kodan). I still remember the day Anish was born. He was the cuddliest little butterball you wanted to squeeze and hug. Ever since he was an infant, he was always so attached to me. I remember during his toddler days, whenever I came home, he would run to the door and excitedly open his arms for me to pick him up. During elementary school, he would always say to me, "You are my best friend, Swati Mosi (maternal aunt)!"

My nephew, Anish Ethan Kodan

Anish is my favorite person in the entire world, and the second funniest person I know (right after his big sister). Today, he is a twenty-year-old college sophomore at University of Maryland College Park. I am so proud of how mature, independent, and responsible he has become since he began college. One important bit of advice I would like to give him is to always hold his own self-respect and never disrespect women. He was raised by so many strong women like his mother, sister, grandmothers, and maternal aunt that he should never forget the value of treating women with dignity. No matter how old he how gets, he will always be my little baby.

A huge acknowledgement and gratitude to my twenty-three-year-old niece, Asha. She has served as the unofficial ghostwriter and editor of *Her Brave Journey*. Asha has reviewed, edited, and rewrote my entire book, as well as my previous blog (mscynicism.com). I may be unapologetically biased, but I do not know anyone in this

world as perfect as Asha. I was sixteen years old when she was born. During that time, I was an emotionally low and insecure teenager. Having Asha come home as an infant with those round apple cheeks, brought much needed joy and laughter to my life, when I needed it most. She was such a fun toy to play with and toss

My niece, Asha Elina Kodan

around! Asha grew up to be such a beautiful, intelligent, and fierce young woman. With her adorable and sarcastic sense of humor, she is the funniest person I know!

She is completing her first year as a medical student at University of Maryland, but to me, she will always be that chubby little baby who used to flap like a bird on the floor when learning how to crawl. I feel so lucky to have her as my niece, and I am overly impressed by the woman she has grown to be. I cannot wait until the day when I address her as Dr. Kodan! I have never longed for children of my own because I have Asha and Anish to fill that void of motherhood. There is nothing in the world their aunt would not do for them.

## SECTION 4 (Friends):

**Bhavna Dhir & Ritu Singh**

Bhavna, Ritu, and I have formed such a strong friendship over the last few years. Ritu and I have been friends since 1996, when we first met at Gaithersburg High School. She has witnessed all the ups and downs I have gone through in the last twenty-five years. I especially appreciate her tough love and transparency. Ritu was the first person to point out that I have a sense of humor and how my unfiltered comments are out of left field!

Bhavna and I met in college but grew close after 2013 when we discovered our mutual love for *The Real Housewives* franchise. She is my Bravo TV buddy! One of my favorite times with Bhavna was when we attended Bravo Con in New York City and snuck into the VIP line for photo ops (that's it?!). Another memorable trip was when we went to the Atlantis in the Bahamas and were thrown around in the wave pool (lol!). Today when we look back, it is one of the funniest stories we commonly share.

Ritu and Bhavna have been so influential in guiding me to make healthier decisions for myself, particularly when I experienced toxic situations. Ritu was the first person I called about one particular toxic situation, even before my family. The best advice she gave me was, "I will support you in whatever decision you make, but I do not want us having this same conversation one year from now." That advice really made me understand that I needed to take action to shape the future I want. I also confided in Bhavna about this same situation, and it became such an emotional moment. Her wisdom, guidance, and compassion have helped me significantly in making healthier choices for myself.

If it were not for these two, I may have stayed in that bad place. I cannot put into words how grateful I am to them both for always being there for me. I love them both with all my heart and look forward to many more fun times, parties, laughter, and hopefully trips once COVID-19 is over!

All the individuals I listed above are my oxygen. I live and breathe because of them and for them. They each have played a significant role in my life, and I hope I have made them proud of the Swati that I am today! Love all of you!! ☺

## SECTION 5:

I want to thank my therapist from the bottom of my heart. When I initially started seeing her, I was a complete mess. She helped me not only understand that my personal situations were toxic, but also encouraged me to see myself more positively. Every Saturday morning, I go to my appointments with my make-up fully done but leave the sessions with my mascara and eyeliner smeared all over my face because her powerful words make me so emotional. Through therapy, I have learned that shedding tears and breaking down my composure is healthy and long overdue. With each therapy session, I have gradually learned to love and respect myself all over again, thanks to her.

## SECTION 6:

Finally, I want to acknowledge John Koehler, Wendolin Perla, Danielle Koehler, and the entire team at Koehler Books for co-publishing *Her Brave Journey*. The first time I talked to Wendolin, she told me that my book made her cry. When I first spoke with John, he wanted to acknowledge the human and emotional aspect of *Her Brave Journey* before talking about the business side of it. That meant a lot to me because it showed that they both felt genuine compassion about my story. I know I annoy the heck out of John with a million questions, so I want to thank him for his patience! I feel incredibly lucky to work with such a strong team of publishing experts. Thank you for selecting me as your business partner. Danielle has done a terrific job designing my author website and advising me on how to maintain it. She is just as talented as her father, John Koehler. I want to also recognize my editors China Cay Cross and Linda Cross of the Cross Literary Agency. Thank you for helping Kiara see that there's forgiveness and kindness in the world.

Last but not the least, a big thank you to my publicist, Bridget Hanretta O'Brien. She has worked extremely hard in helping me promote *Her Brave Journey* and did such an amazing job. We extensively worked side-by-side, and I thoroughly enjoyed this collaborative journey.

Looking at all the amazing individuals in my acknowledgements, I feel truly blessed to be surrounded by such a strong support system. Whether it is those who raised, loved, mentored, or professionally collaborated with me, it really does take a village to shape the published author I am privileged to be today.